COMPREHENDING COINCIDENCE

COMPREHENDING COINCIDENCE

SYNCHRONICITY AND PERSONAL TRANSFORMATION

Craig S. Bell

CHRYSALIS BOOKS • WEST CHESTER, PENNSYLVANIA

Library of Congress Cataloging-in-Publication Data
Bell, Craig S.
    Comprehending coincidence : synchronicity
and personal transformation / Craig S. Bell.
      p. cm.
    Includes bibliographical references and index.
    ISBN 0-87785-393-2
    1. Coincidence. I. Title.

    BF1175.B45 2000
    133—dc21   00-043103

Acknowledgments
Excerpts from *The Collected Works of C. G. Jung* are reprinted by
permission of Princeton University Press.
Excerpts from *The Complete Works of Swami Vivekananda* are
reprinted by permission of Advaita Ashrama. Calcutta, India.
Rumi's "The Dream That Must Be Interpreted," translated by
Coleman Barks, was originally published by Threshold Books.

Edited by Betty Christiansen
Design by Gopa Design and Illustration
Set in Minion
Printed in the United States of America.

Chrysalis Books is an imprint of the Swedenborg
Foundation, Inc. For more information, contact:
Swedenborg Foundation Publishers
320 North Church Street
West Chester, PA 19380
or
http://www.swedenborg.com.

To
My Love
Wendy

Contents

Introduction

I don't know if we each have a destiny
or if we're all just floating around,
accidental, like on a breeze.
                    Forrest Gump

In 1838, Edgar Allen Poe published a story entitled *The Narrative of Arthur Gordon Pym of Nantucket*. In the story, four shipwreck survivors are adrift in an open boat. One of the four is a cabin boy named Richard Parker. The other three survivors kill Richard Parker. And then they eat him.

Forty-six years later, in real life, three men were on trial in London. They had been shipwrecked and had remained adrift together in a lifeboat. They were on trial for the murder of a fourth man in that boat, whom they had killed and then ate. The fourth man was a cabin boy. His name was Richard Parker.

At the trial of the three men, the coincidence of the actual events replicating the fictitious incident was noted. Apparently, none of the three knew of the Edgar Allen Poe story, so it cannot be said to have influenced their actions. In 1973, this remarkable alignment of fiction and fact won a contest for the best coincidence in the London *Sunday Times* (Vaughan 1979, 22).

This shocking coincidence seems to point to destiny or fate. Even the most committed skeptic cannot attribute such a dramatic alignment of fiction and fact—right down to the victim's name—to accident.

Most coincidences are not so clearcut. With most, a cynic may claim there's a good chance it's just chance.

In World War II, a couple of young West Virginians were best buddies in their battalion. They served together in Holland toward the end of the war. It was there, in February of 1945, that one of them was shredded by forty-two fragments of shrapnel from a German land mine. His friend mourned the death of his buddy, but death was the companion of those in the war, so life went on with "X," only an occasional glance back in remembrance.

Over fifty years later, in a factory town on the shores of Lake Erie, two elderly men were waiting in a doctor's office for relatives who were being treated. They struck up a conversation. Soon mention of the war was made. Once it was established that they both had served, they began to compare notes. They were surprised to find they had been in the same antiaircraft battalion. The one asked the other if any of his buddies were fatalities. He mentioned "Little Red."

"I hate to disappoint you," the white-haired man next to him responded, "but I'm very much alive."

Alhough his dog tags had been removed while he lay on the battlefield—which was considered a pronouncement of death—Little Red had survived that day and over fifty years since. The two buddies from West Virginia had lived in that same northern Ohio town for two decades, where neither knew of the other's existence until that surprising day in the doctor's office, when the dead came alive and the image two men had had of each other, as brash twenty-one-year-olds, received a fast-forward of fifty years (The New Haven *Register*, 1996).

Are such events accident or destiny? That question does not apply only to rare and dramatic twists of fate. It is also pondered in regard to the more common coincidences many of us encounter. They too may leave us with a strong sense that the alignment of events is not just chance.

Most people feel there really is something to coincidences, that they are not merely accidental, but meaningful, perhaps even instructional. Yet that recognition alone has a similar effect as the aroma of a freshly baked apple pie: It awakens the appetite but doesn't satisfy it.

Coincidences prick our curiosity and our sense of wonder, yet we're usually not sure how to treat them. This is because they don't appear to be governed by the cause-and-effect relationship we use to explain the flow of most events about us. Your radiant smile causes another to smile back; flicking the switch causes the light to come on. These sequences are simple and logical. But how do you explain the fact that, just as you were thinking about your ex-lover, you stopped at a traffic light behind a car with a license plate that precisely displayed the numerals for the month, day, and year of his birth? Not only are we mystified about the hidden mechanisms in our world that can produce such a simultaneous connection, we are often just as much in the dark when it comes to recognizing the meaning of coincidences.

The good news is that the cloak concealing the significance of coincidental events may be removed without much difficulty. Then, we find revealed not just meaning, but often wisdom and guidance as well.

The purpose of many books is simply to entertain—to delight and excite. You'll certainly find this investigation of coincidence entertaining, and interesting as well. But it will also give you something you can take with you, something that will make your life more entertaining, more interesting, and more fruitful.

The coincidences we'll examine here are real, the types of coincidences you might encounter in your own life. Most examples in this book were experienced by my friends, my relatives, or myself. Many are dramatic. Others are rather subtle, and could even go unnoticed. They, too, are important. The coincidence itself may not always be what is most interesting, and it's certainly not what is most important. Its meaning is what is most important, and perhaps most interesting, too. While a coincidence can be over in an instant, its meaning may last a lifetime. We'll take a good look at how to analyze the meaning of coincidences—both startling and subtle—but we'll go beyond that. We'll determine when the meaning is actually useful and how to use it. We are most concerned with the process of extracting and then applying the meaning of the coincidences we encounter.

How do we begin to use coincidences to help us achieve

fulfillment and contentment? The first step may be to recognize that, as Einstein said, "God does not throw dice." Nothing happens by accident. Modern science in general, and nuclear physics in particular, has come to the realization that all the phenomena about us are interwoven and interconnected. This is not a new discovery. The mystics of all religions have long held the perspective that everything in our world is part of one grand, interactive whole. This one divine consciousness manifesting as all of creation may be termed the Tao or Brahman in the East, while in the West, we may know it as God.

So we start with the premise that all coincidences are meaningful. In fact, as I interpret it, coincidences are meaningful by definition. *Webster's Third New International Dictionary* says that, in addition to not conforming to the law of cause and effect, coincidence consists of "the concurrence of events or circumstances appropriate to one another or having significance in relationship to one another." As I see it, to say that events or circumstances are appropriate to each other or have a significant relationship to each other is to say their arrangement is meaningful. Most important, though, my experience and investigation of coincidence have shown this to be true.

My investigation of coincidence began more than twenty-five years ago. It evolved from my interest in psychology, which was my college major. In college, I was intrigued by Carl Jung's insights on the dynamics of the human mind. I was dismayed to see systems such as Freud's psychoanalysis, with its emphasis on hidden sexual motives, or Skinner's mechanistic behaviorism receive more serious and thorough treatment than Jung's deeper, more balanced, and more complete view of reality, which stretched the boundaries of science.

After college, I became an Air Force pilot. It was while stationed at Cam Rahn Bay Air Base, on the shores of the South China Sea in Vietnam, that I took out a book from the base library that changed my life. The book was *Man and His Symbols,* by Carl Jung and associates. *Man and His Symbols* is basically about humankind's unconscious mind and the symbols used to express its view of reality in dreams and other areas of life: myths, art, literature, film, and so on. The book was so pregnant with new and exciting perspectives that sometimes I'd only read one page at a sitting, then put it aside to digest the fruit of Jung's exploration of the unconscious realm.

Jung said the sometimes incomprehensible symbols of our dreams are not just nonsense, but contain real truths about ourselves. Soon after I began analyzing the motley and sometimes bizarre imagery of my dreams, I was astonished to find that the meaning they concealed conveyed logical and practical information about my true nature. When I subsequently analyzed others' dreams, I found that the dreamer would sometimes emit a spontaneous and gratifying "ah, yes," when the meaning of a poignant symbol or dream sequence was deciphered. Eventually, a modest book on dream analysis was written at the request of a writer/publisher friend.

In a dream, one setting or situation may be instantly replaced by another, then another, and another, each seemingly unrelated. Yet careful examination of the symbolic content may reveal an underlying theme common to them all, of which each segment is a variant. Once I recognized this underlying continuity of dream sequences, I wondered if viewing life through the same lens could help decode some of its mysteries. A series of apparently unrelated chance situations may, in retrospect, appear to have all served in various ways to bring about a specific result, recognition, or life situation. Coincidences are particularly dramatic examples of the power of these seemingly random events. So to me, the investigation of coincidence seemed an appropriate and interesting means of assessing whether seemingly fortuitous circumstances possess deeper meaning.

The dominant philosophical perspectives of both India and China have for thousands of years viewed the particular circumstances encountered by a person at any point in life as somehow merited and appropriate. In China, this perception has long been exemplified by a classic book on philosophy and divination known as the *I Ching* (the Classic of Flowing Change), which in the past few decades has also become well known in the Western world.[1]

Carl Jung wrote the forward to Richard Wilhelm's rendering of the *I Ching*, which is the most popular version in the West. There, Jung explained the premise underlying the *I Ching* as it relates to the one consulting it for guidance: "Synchronicity [Jung's term for coincidence] takes the coincidence of events in space and time as meaning something more than mere chance, namely, a peculiar interdependence of objective events among themselves as well as with the subjective (psychic) states of the observer or observers." (Wilhelm 1967, xxiv)

What is significant here is Jung's recognition that coincidental events possess a peculiar interdependence with the subjective state of the observer. This is the central and singular most important fact about coincidences. A coincidence is always appropriate and relevant to the person(s) encountering it, and it often is a reflection of the psychological state of the person at the time it occurs. Later on, we'll look at many examples of coincidences that will help clarify this fact.

The evolution of my long-standing relationship with coincidence was thus stimulated by a few key factors: First was the discovery of meaning in seemingly unrelated and sometimes bizarre dream events, leading to the conjecture that some of the unpredictable, apparently chance events of life might also be meaningfully arranged. This hypothesis was bolstered by the philosophical foundations of the *I Ching*, particularly Chinese Taoism's traditional view that seemingly random occurrences are related and appropriate to our state of being—a part of the grand and mysterious flow of the Tao. Jung's observations on coincidence (synchronicity), particularly those extracted from his *Collected Works*

---

1. The usual method of consulting the *I Ching* consists of taking three coins, assigning the number two to one side and three to the other, and tossing the coins together six times while focusing upon a particular question. The series of tosses will produce a sequence of odd and even numbers, of which there are sixty-four different possibilities, each one being associated with a particular decision or answer. The specific one received is considered to be appropriate to the question focused upon when the coins are tossed.

and presented in a small book simply entitled *Synchronicity*, also provided considerable impetus. These factors, and an intuitive sense of hidden meaning, induced me to become engaged in an ongoing effort to probe the mysterious shroud of coincidence, seeking its true nature.

The investigation of coincidence is a natural choice in seeking a hidden connectedness within the forces that buffet us, for the frequently dramatic nature of coincidences not only grabs our attention, it highlights the possibility of deeper meaning in life. My approach has been to postulate tentative meanings for coincidences encountered by myself or associates, then to see if the interpretations can be verified by present circumstances or future developments. Over time, this allows meaningfulness to be empirically validated or refuted.

As I see it, there are basically two types of coincidences. The first type I refer to as *mirror coincidences*, for they *reflect* a focus of the mind that is highly charged with energy. If a person is gripped by a great concern or burning desire, a coincidence may occur that directly mirrors that intense concern.

The meaning of a coincidence is determined in a similar manner as a competent analyst determines the meaning of events in a dream. There are many parallels between dreams and coincidences. Most dreams are the creative, dynamic expression of aspects of the conscious or unconscious mind that are charged with energy. Mirror coincidences function like dreams in that the coincidental circumstances reflect highly energized concerns of the mind. We'll look at sufficient examples of different types of mirror coincidences to reveal how they operate and—in a completely logical process—how meaning is determined.

The other basic type of coincidence, *directional coincidence*, is also generally related to one's state of mind. However, directional coincidences are associated more with an open receptivity to guidance and are the product of an intelligence that is far superior than our own: an all-knowing supraconsciousness, rather than our limited awareness. Directional coincidences occur to provide each of us with particular guidance for contentment and fulfillment appropriate to our own journey through life. The rationale behind directional coincidences, their importance, their meaning, and their use are the primary focus of this book.

If we accept that coincidences are meaningful, it would be relatively easy to use them effectively if only their meanings were simple to establish. Therein lies the challenge. For like dreams, coincidences frequently express meaning symbolically. An ability to analyze symbols is, therefore, important to determine meaning. Yet the good news is that symbol analysis is not difficult. And it's fun. A few simple rules can be used successfully by nearly everyone for the quite logical process of symbol analysis. Other similarities between dreams and coincidences, as well as additional tools for postulating and verifying meaning, will also be examined.

It is no accident that dreams and coincidences adhere to the same rules. In fact, philosophers of the East have long maintained that life is dreamlike. And in the West, many physicists have come to share that realization.

The *Yoga Vasistha*, a respected classic of India, says: "Creation is a dream. The waking state is a dream. Even though this creation or world appearance is apparently seen and experienced, it is in reality the realization of the notions that arise in us" (Venkatesananda 1993, 673). Elsewhere, it states: "Even as the objects seem to exist and function in the inner world of consciousness in a dream, objects seem to exist and function in the outer world of consciousness during the wakeful state. . . . Even as consciousness alone is the reality in the dream state, consciousness alone is the substance in the wakeful state too" (367).

Rumi, the great thirteenth-century Sufi poet, perceives life as "The Dream that Must Be Interpreted":

> This place is a dream.
> Only a sleeper considers it real.
> Then death comes like dawn,
> and you wake up laughing
> at what you thought was your grief. (Barks 1997, 112)

On a lighter note, we may look to the famous Chinese Taoist Chuang Tzu, of the fourth century BCE:

Once, I Chuang Chou dreamed that I was a butterfly and was happy as a butterfly. I was conscious that I was quite pleased with myself, but I did not know that I was Chou. Suddenly I awoke, and there I was, visibly Chou. I do not know if it was Chou dreaming that he was a butterfly or the butterfly dreaming that it was Chou. (Chan 1963, 190)

In *Mysticism and the New Physics*, Michael Talbot says of John Wheeler, a respected physicist who began his career at Princeton, "Wheeler's conception of quantum interconnectedness . . . makes our universe into an immense dream space. That is, our perceptions of space and time in a dream exist only to the extent that we conceive them. . . . In a dream, as in Wheeler's superspace, all points in dream space and dream time are ultimately connected to all other points via the dreamer" (Talbot 1981, 89).

In the following pages, we'll see quite clearly that in some instances, at least with coincidences, our physical world behaves quite like the world of dreams. I am not simply speaking of the fact that, like dreams, coincidences often convey meaning symbolically or that, like dreams, as we will see, coincidences are frequently a result of the focus of psychological energy in some sphere of concern. I am also referring to the fact that, as with dreams, the rules that normally govern our physical worlds are ignored or transcended by coincidences. The barriers of time and space, and the formidable, solidified nature of the material world take on the character of a dream fantasy—a fantasy that is shaped according to the dictates of our own minds or the power of a supraconsciousness.

These perceptions are increasingly coming to enjoy a dual verification. As a scientist might say, their truth is recognized both intuitively and empirically. In other words, what we strongly sense to be true is also proven to be true.

We sense that both the dramatic coincidences that compel our attention and the more frequent subtle coincidences that sometimes escape our notice are not accidental, but are somehow meaningfully arranged. In addition to our intuitive awareness of meaning, scientists are finding ever-increasing evidence that this is true.

The mechanistic worldview of yesterday's scientist has been unmasked. Science of late increasingly echoes the mystic's clear understanding that everything in our world is interconnected, interrelated, and interactive. Everything—including each of us—is in essence, and in a quite practical sense, part of the same whole—the same being. As physicist Fritjof Capra observed in *The Tao of Physics:* "In modern physics the universe is thus experienced as a dynamic, inseparable whole which always includes the observer in an essential way. In this experience, the traditional concepts of space and time, of isolated objects, and of cause and effect, lose their meaning" (Capra 1991, 81).

Suppose, for a moment, that you and I grew up with a tribe of bushmen in Africa. Then, after we had attained adulthood, with the same intelligence we now enjoy, we were whisked to a home in the "civilized world" for the first time. Our hosts, who spoke a different language, placed us in a large room with soft things to sit on. After a while, we noticed that there was a tall narrow box against a wall that every now and then went *bong, bong, bong.* And every time, right after it did, something else in another room answered with *cuckoo, cuckoo, cuckoo.* We, being quite intelligent, realized the tall thing going *bong* caused the other thing to go *cuckoo.* Not knowing what a clock is, this conclusion is quite logical. However, since we did not grow up with a tribe of bushmen, we know the first clock was set or running a little faster than the second, thus only appeared to cause the other to respond to it.

The scientist and the mystic say that some of our perceptions of reality are subject to similar misconceptions. For hundreds of thousands of years, humans knew that the sun rose in the morning, traveled across the sky during the day, and set in the evening. It was just a few hundred years ago that Galileo discovered that the earth revolved and rotated around the sun; the sun only *appeared* to revolve about the earth. We still experience the sun as rising in the morning and setting in the evening, and still describe it in those terms, although we now know that is not what is happening. In similar fashion, modern physics has revealed the misconceptions of classical science. As Capra pointed out, "the traditional concepts of space and time, of isolated objects, and of cause and effect, lose their meaning."

It is not necessary to explore the deeper metaphysical basis of coincidence (hinted at in the last few pages) in order to know how we influence its occurrence, or to comprehend its meaning and practical application. Yet some readers will want a clearer understanding of how our physical world can generate the spontaneous emergence of meaningful coincidences. So, in the last chapter, we'll seek, and I believe find, answers to that question.

Sometimes, we feel unfulfilled, yet don't know what we want out of life. We feel there's something lacking, but don't know what it is. Then, it may turn out that, even when we think we know what we need and passionately yearn for it, even pray for it, when we ultimately get what we are seeking, we are still left unfulfilled, perhaps even more miserable than we were before.

This is where coincidences come in. When we are caught up in the drama and intensity of our own plans and schemes, our own imperfect recipe for the banquet of life, coincidences occur that mirror, for better or worse, that which grips us. Contentment is assured only when we shed our layers of immediate "needs" and our limited vision to open ourselves up to the far greater intelligence that permeates all of creation and knows to perfection the particular things that we each—individually—need for enrichment and happiness. Then coincidences occur that direct us along the particular path appropriate for each of our personal journeys in this lifetime. The more we are open and receptive to guidance, the more profuse and profound the direction will be.

Each life has a purpose. All of life is an educational experience, and the world we inhabit is our classroom. Our purpose, in lifetime after lifetime, is to draw ever closer to the unlimited potential that we each possess within our own being. If we will only open ourselves up to learning, the situations we encounter will instruct us. This is the practical value of the many subtle and dramatic coincidences that may guide us on our journey toward completeness, fulfillment, and enduring contentment. To profit, we must merely dispense with our restricted and biased perspectives and open ourselves up to the direction that is being presented to us in our everyday world.

You are invited to become a student of life—a student of *your own* life, so that you may realize your own highest potential for harmony and contentment. My intent is to open your awareness to the very practical tools coincidence provides, which may be employed toward achieving that goal.

COMPREHENDING COINCIDENCE

 Mirror
Coincidence

Passages

FOR FORTY-ODD YEARS, a man has awakened early in the morning, bathed, eaten, gotten in his car, and headed off to work. Day in and day out, week after week, year upon year, for eight, nine, ten hours at a time, earning a living. A wife to come home to at night, and children who have come, been reared, and gone. Crises also have come and gone, leaving remnants behind. Grandchildren to love, a wife interred, a new bride. Through it all—all the ups and downs—getting up in the morning to go off to work and returning in the evening with a day's work done. Assignments have changed, even companies, but the essential routine has remained. It has been the prison and the sanctuary, a constant, a provider of self-worth and meaning.

Finally, the last workday arrives. Associates wish him well: "Good luck," "Enjoy your freedom." His desk is cleaned out; he shakes hands and receives embraces. Then, as is traditional there, he is escorted to his car by his coworkers, who cheer and yell and bang on anything they can find to make noise. It is 2:30 in the afternoon. Later, he happens to check the time on his watch. He is surprised to see that it has stopped, even though a jeweler put in a new battery the previous week. The watch reads 2:30.

A couple of years ago, my stepfather encountered the events

related here. At the exact time he left work for the last time, his watch stopped. What makes this coincidence dramatic is not so much the coincidental event itself, but rather its particular relationship with the highly charged situation with which it is simultaneous: the end of the work phase of life and beginning of retirement.

In relation to work, a timepiece is a potent symbol. Its stopping at the same time my stepfather's career ended provides a many-faceted metaphor and a clear mirror coincidence. For all those years, he had to get up at a certain time, leave home at a specific time, have lunch at a particular time, quit at a definite time. The period of time in which his life was dictated by time went on for a long time. That time stopped, just when the watch stopped. The necessity to monitor time also stopped, now freeing him from that constraint.

On the other hand, that which had provided meaning, focus, a sense of self-worth, respectability, and productivity, also stopped with the last exit from the workplace. With all those hours occupied at work now ended, what would he do with his time? Would time stand still?

Retirement from work is one of life's major transitions, like the first day of school, graduation, marriage, childbirth, or a new career. These are more or less universal situations, which nearly everyone encounters, generation after generation, in cultures all over the world. There is a universal complex—a kind of blueprint, archetype, or pattern of thoughts, feelings, and emotions—that we each possess for these passages in life. These patterns, when highly energized, may be reflected in coincidences. Certainly, the retirement complex was fully charged right when my stepfather's watch stopped.

In the introduction, I identified two types of coincidences, the first of which was termed a mirror coincidence. In a mirror coincidence, the coincidental events—often in dramatic fashion—reflect or mirror a current dominant concern of the psyche (the conscious and unconscious mind). A mirror coincidence does not provide us with guidance or direction. For the most part, it does not provide us with much new information about ourselves, and it might not change our life situation at all. On the other hand, our personal world may change dramatically to reflect the content of the charged area of focus or concern that the coincidence mirrors.

The stopping of my stepfather's watch at the exact time of his final departure from work is a classic example of mirror coincidence. The watch's stopping provided no direction or guidance. It merely reflected a part of my stepfather's (conscious and unconscious) mind that was highly charged with energy. Had he analyzed the symbolic significance of this coincidence, the circumstances it reflected would not have provided much new information for him. He was aware of his increased freedom from time constraints. He was also aware of and anxious about the lack of structure, the lack of validation, and the excess of free time he would have on his hands.

One of the emotionally charged, usually unconscious thoughts present in the retirement complex is that there is only one stage of life left following retirement. That is the death of the body. It is not uncommon for very healthy people, at the time of retirement, to have vivid dreams of the grim reaper paying a visit. My stepfather, too, entertained the possibility that his watch's stopping might be a foreshadowing of death.

In fact, there have been numerous authenticated instances, mirror coincidences, wherein a clock stopped at the exact moment of death. One of the better-known examples is Frederick the Great's death, when the pendulum clock in the palace at San Souci stopped. However, such a coincidence is simultaneous with death; it does not foreshadow death. Yet, in one respect, my stepfather's experience does symbolize and coincide with death: the death or cessation of a phase of his life and a part of his identity: the death of the working man.

In a mirror coincidence such as this, once we've identified the dominant concern being reflected, we might stop to ponder what, if anything, we've gained with our newfound knowledge. After all, we've noted that mirror coincidences do not provide us with guidance on how to proceed in life.

Yet, on a subtle level, a sensitive person may see some significance in a mirror coincidence. This is the awareness that one's life is not a solitary thread, slowly unwound until just the bare wooden spool remains, but is interwoven in the grand, multicolored tapestry of ongoing creation. We recognize that, somehow, the things that happen to us and around us in our small sphere of existence are interrelated and meaningful in the context of our own unfolding drama. And we sense it all might possess a greater significance than we dare hope for. The guidance we are given is to be more considerate, to consider more about each of our little worlds and our appropriate roles within them.

It is also beneficial to have the ability to identify mirror coincidences just so we have a better handle on what is behind the sometimes mysterious and confusing course of events in our lives. The ability to identify and analyze mirror coincidences provides us with a greater capacity to understand the meaning of important incidents whose significance might otherwise elude us. And since they reflect a charged component of our mind, the most immediate consequence is a better understanding of ourselves and the sometimes deeply hidden things that might grip us.

Finally, it is important to have the capacity to identify mirror coincidences simply so that we do not mistake them for the more important and more frequent, though frequently less dramatic, directional coincidences that *do* offer us guidance on how best to proceed with life. We certainly do not want to be looking for guidance where there is none provided.

THE COMPLEX AS AN ELECTROMAGNET

Before we investigate more mirror coincidences, we ought to take a closer look at the rules they follow. In doing so, it would be helpful to refer to Carl Jung's observations about synchronicity.

Synchronicity is essentially just another name for *coincidence.* In fact, Jung's definition of synchronicity as "meaningful coincidence" appears redundant, since coincidence is—as I read it—by definition meaningful. Furthermore, inasmuch as coincidence is also by definition not a function of the law of cause and effect, Jung's reference to it as "an acausal connecting principle" suffers similarly.[1] For those reasons, I have chosen to omit the use of the term *synchronicity* in this book to identify what in reality is simply coincidence.[2]

Yet because coincidence and synchronicity are essentially the same, Jung's observations about synchronicity are equally valid for coincidence. In addition, because my investigation of coincidence was partially the result of Jung's work on synchronicity, and since the symbol analysis and observations on human psychology presented here are indebted to and consistent with Jungian (analytical) psychology, it is appropriate and useful to take a look at some of Jung's conclusions.

Jung made an important statement about synchronicity that might sound confusing, although its meaning may actually be deciphered without much difficulty. He said, "Synchronicity designates the parallelism of time and meaning between psychic and psychophysical events" (Jung 1973, 115). First, let's substitute *coincidence* for *synchronicity*. By *psychic event,* Jung means one that occurs in the psyche, which is the totality of the psychological self, consisting of the conscious mind and the very vast, sometimes turbulent reservoir of the unconscious. The physical events of a coincidence are identified as being not merely physical but

---

1. According to *Webster's Third New International Dictionary*, coincidence is "the concurrence of events or circumstances appropriate to one another or having significance in relation to one another but between which there is no casual connection."

2. Additional objections to the term *synchronicity* are presented by Arthur Koestler in *The Roots of Coincidence*: "Jung's concept of synchronicity seems to refer only to simultaneous events—although he includes precognitive dreams which occurred sometimes several days before the events. He tried to get around the time paradox by saying that the unconscious mind functions outside of the physical framework of space-time; thus precognitive experiences are 'evidently not synchronous but synchronistic since they are experienced as psychic images in the present as though the objective event already existed.' One wonders why Jung created these unnecessary complications by coining a term which implies simultaneity, and then explaining that it does not mean what it means."

psychophysical; in other words, meaningfully related to the psyche or the psychological self.

The events of a coincidence, in addition to being meaningfully connected to each other, are also meaningfully connected to the individual encountering the coincidence—to his or her state of mind. This is what gives the events their "psychophysical" classification. This is also the reason (just as with dream analysis) we always look at the primary aspects of the individual's physical and psychological situation when seeking meaning.

Here is a minor coincidence that provides an excellent example of what is meant by a psychophysical event: My wife suggested that an example would be helpful here, but neither one of us could think of one that satisfied us. Yet the very next day, by coincidence, she witnessed the following sequence of events that provide an excellent illustration of a psychophysical event.

A flight attendant was serving passengers from one of those rabbit-in-the-hat type carts from which an unending array of things seems to materialize. While she was attending to the needs of one row of passengers, another passenger from behind repeatedly tapped her on the shoulder. One would naturally expect this to irritate her. Still, a moment or two later, when the irritating passenger was served, the flight attendant merely took a can of soda from the cart and provided it and a snack with no expression of the displeasure that was brewing within. When the passenger opened the can of soda (although it hadn't been handled differently from any other can) a minor geyser unexpectedly erupted, spewing liquid upon the deserving passenger.

If we assume the pent-up force in the can of soda reflected the pent-up agitation of the flight attendant toward the passenger, then the eruption of the soda may be considered a psychophysical event. The psychological state of the flight attendant, in being meaningfully connected to and reflected in the physical event, made the latter a psychophysical event—and the set of circumstances a coincidence.

It is very important to understand how heightened or charged concerns of the mind influence both our perceptions of our personal environment and what actually happens in it. Once we are familiar with the relationship between the mind and the situations that may be encountered when a component of the mind is, in effect, magnetized, we will be able to see how coincidences are related to mental states.

Most of us have one or more areas of interest toward which we concentrate a great deal of our mental (and physical) energy. For a single mother, these could be her occupation and her child. For a married father, these might be his occupation, his wife, his children, and his golf game. Our mental energy is not divided equally between these central areas of concern, nor does it remain at a constant level for any particular one. It will vary greatly with factors such as the time of day, whether there is a crisis in an area, or whether an area is providing a lot of pleasure or reward. On Saturday, for the married father, it may be that in the morning, the psychic center for golf is charged with energy; in the afternoon, the psychic center for children is charged; and in the evening, the center for wife and lover is charged.

For the single mother, if there is a crisis at work, the psychic center of her mind for that area may be charged with a great deal of energy for days or weeks. If there is a serious problem with her child, almost all of her mental energy may be consumed by that psychic center for an extended period. On the other hand, if she is not involved in a romantic relationship and longs for one, that psychic center may be highly charged—perhaps even without her being aware of it.

Let's look at a hypothetical situation. Suppose you once had an intense love affair with someone you worked with at a summer camp. On your first date, the two of you hitchhiked into town and were picked up by a driver in a vintage Mustang convertible. Your lover was a "Trekkie," so, after you moved in together, you both watched *Star Trek* whenever it was on. You both enjoyed going to the Thai restaurant that was around the corner from the apartment you shared. Your final argument was over whether you were considerate enough of your lover's feelings.

Psychic centers tend to behave like an electromagnet. When the power is turned on—when charged—it tends to attract things. Experiences that occur when a psychological situation is energized will remain associated with that situation. Even if the charge is greatly reduced, activities and experiences will remain associated with the psychic center—the situation—to which they've been attached.

After your love affair was over, you avoided Thai restaurants, hated *Star Trek* with a passion, and got an uneasy feeling whenever you saw an old Mustang convertible. God forbid that anyone even hinted you were inconsiderate. Yet now that you are secure in a new relationship, when the topic of summer camp comes up, for instance, in a movie or TV show, or if you notice an old Mustang convertible, a smile comes to your face because they remind you of your old love when it was idyllic and new.

The emotional love affair served as a charged magnet that caused other objects and situations around it to be attached to it and remain associated with it, to form a complex (an association of related things often in intricate combination). The different elements of the complex came to have the power to represent and elicit the emotionally charged psychic center to which they had become attached. In this situation, *Star Trek*, vintage Mustang convertibles, Thai restaurants, and accusations of insensitivity all became attached to the emotionally charged "intense love/painful separation" psychic center to form an enduring complex of electrified interwoven circumstances.

Jung introduced the concept of complexes. In his conception, "a complex is an organized group or constellation of feelings, thoughts, perceptions, and memories which exists in the personal unconscious. It has a nucleus which acts as a kind of magnet attracting to it or 'constellating' various experiences" (Hall and Lindzey, 1963, 79).

In Jung's original framework, the complex monopolized an excessively high proportion of mental energy and was indicative of individuals suffering from neurotic or psychotic problems. Such an individual related nearly everything he or she encountered to the perspective of the enormous complex. One with a power complex (such as Hitler) views everything with the goal of personal power or supremacy in mind. One with a mother complex will be influenced by either conscious or unconscious perceptions of one's mother's approval, disapproval, likes, dislikes, thoughts, and so on.

Jung came to see, and I think we can agree, that all normal people have complexes of psychic energy interwoven with a core component. The complex may be general (work, romantic love, parenthood, school, sports) or specific (Reliable Realty Corp, my affair with Pat, my youngest child, Amity High School, Little League Baseball) or a combination of both. Although the complex as a whole may be said to reside in the unconscious, we are aware of many of its components, and most are at least accessible to the conscious mind. A particular complex also has the capacity to become dominant for a period of time, perhaps to become a ravenous monster complex with enormous energy, although we might not even be aware that it is lurking within and without. As Jung noted, when emotionally charged, these cores of psychic energy attract to themselves experiences that happen to occur around them. These experiences continue to be closely associated with the core circumstance even after the complex is much less energized. In addition, the previously neutral events and experiences become so firmly associated with the core situation that any of them may spontaneously evoke many of the same feelings, memories, and emotions—for example, Thai restaurants symbolizing your "intense love/painful separation" complex. They have become symbols for the core situation, with nearly the same psychic power as the original nucleus.

Our interest in complexes is in their role in mirror coincidences. The conclusion I have arrived at regarding mirror coincidences is that events previously attached to the nucleus of the complex—things that have come to represent the core situation—may spontaneously appear in one's environment when the core component is charged. These, therefore, provide us with a coincidence that mirrors the complex or key aspects of it.

For example, let us say that, while sharing a light dinner with your new lover, a minor misunderstanding arises, in which you are accused of being insensitive. In anger and anguish, when that still-vulnerable nerve is struck, you abruptly get up and escape to the adjoining living room, where you plunk down and click on the television. The program on television just happens to be a rerun of *Star Trek*. After a moment, you realize with horror that it is the exact same episode you and your ex-lover were watching when you had the heated final argument about your insensitivity.

This is a mirror coincidence. First, the insensitivity issue is raised, which activates the "intense love/painful separation" complex, immediately followed by a coincidence that symbolically reflects the complex: the unexpected encounter with the ill-fated *Star Trek* episode.

We should digress here a little bit to introduce briefly the other major type of coincidence. It goes beyond mirroring the already existing content of the mind to provide direction on how to proceed, or whether to proceed, in a given situation. This type of coincidence—directional coincidence—may encourage, discourage, or even prevent a particular course of behavior.

My wife, Wendy, related the following dramatic directional coincidence, which happened to her cousin. One evening when she was in her late teens, Wendy's cousin was riding through town with some friends when she happened to notice some other friends of hers. After stopping to say hello, she ended up staying with them instead of continuing with the friends she had been with. Minutes later, all her previous companions were killed in a tragic auto accident.

We've all heard of situations like this: ones in which some unforseen circumstance arises to dissuade someone from doing what she or he intended to do, thereby saving the person's life. Certainly, the vast majority of directional coincidences are not so dramatic. This will become evident when we investigate them in chapter two, where our focus is not on lifesaving directional coincidences, but rather those that are life-guiding.

Now let's take another look at your "intense love/painful separation" coincidence to see if it may provide some direction. If you look closely at the circumstance of encountering the specific *Star Trek* episode immediately after the insensitivity issue was raised by your new love, you might suspect that there is more going on here than just the mirroring of circumstances you are already aware of. I would tend to agree.

This coincidence may have extended beyond the mirror category into the directional category. Its purpose may have been to make a point. You might find it prudent to take a real, open look at yourself. Is this coincidence encouraging you, directing you, to work toward becoming a more sensitive and compassionate person, which would help preserve and strengthen your love relationship? It is likely that is the case.

If it is a directional coincidence we are investigating, we also need to know how to put it to work for us. Again, how one verifies the meaning of a coincidence is similar to how one verifies the meaning of a dream: you test your conclusion, or your hypothesis, with your awareness of reality.

Suppose you conclude your insensitivity coincidence might be directing you to exhibit more sensitivity in relating to the people around you, in particular, to your lover. You openly look at your past behavior to see if there are significant instances where you might have been insensitive to the needs or feelings of your friends and relations. After doing so, you concede that, in fact, you can identify some marked instances in which you could have been more sensitive. You tentatively approach your lover, conceding that perhaps you could be more sensitive, and ask for an opinion on how and where you should be more sympathetic and receptive in your mutual relationship and in your relationships with others.

In the following weeks, after you have consistently made an effort to be more sensitive, you are pleased to note your relationships with your lover, and with your friends and relations, seem more intimate, open, and satisfying than ever. So, we can see that, through a number of measures, you have tested your interpretation of the meaning of the coincidence with practical reality, implemented your conclusions, and received verification that they were valid.

The most important consideration in responding to your interpretation of the meaning of a coincidence is to proceed with caution and tentatively. We do not effect substantial changes in our lifestyle unless our interpretation of the guidance a coincidence has provided makes sense to us. It must be reinforced by an objective appraisal of our situation and the options open to us. And then, when we do proceed, we continuously evaluate the appropriateness of the steps being taken along the way.

This is particularly important when the content of the coincidence is highly symbolic. We want to be sure that our interpretation of symbolic content is correct. As we will see later in this chapter, with "The Case of the Wayward Bicycles" (and more fully when we address the subject of symbol analysis in detail in chapter three), symbol analysis proceeds quite logically. Nevertheless, many symbols may have various meanings, so we want to be sure the meaning we attribute to the symbol is the correct one. This, of course, is most important when acting upon the guidance provided by directional coincidences. Yet even the meaning perceived to be reflected in mirror coincidences may be acted upon in subtle and not-so-subtle ways. Here, too, we want to be confident our interpretation of meaning is correct.

THE NAME OF LOVE

Coincidences unfold in a totally free and uninhibited manner, without conformity to any rules except one: that the coincidence is meaningfully related to the one encountering it. Additionally, with a mirror coincidence, a charged complex will be at play. One of the more unusual coincidences I have heard of was experienced by my next-door neighbor, Shawn. Yet once the charged complex was identified, hers could be classified as a pretty standard mirror coincidence.

My neighbor has had two boyfriends in her life. She dated the first one from about age fourteen until graduation from college. His first name was Dave. Dave didn't like his last name, and sometimes said he wished he could change it. He liked the sound of a particular name that he said he would like to have as his last name.

After she had broken up with Dave, Shawn moved about 1,300 miles south, from her native New England to vibrant Miami.

There, while hanging out at the beach one day with her visiting mother, watching a variety of men pass by—no doubt with her "true love" complex highly energized—she spontaneously exhibited some uncharacteristic behavior. She hailed a couple of good-looking guys ambling by with scuba gear in hand. The two were eager to stop and chat.

She started dating one of the young men, and eventually—after they'd been going together for only about nine years—they got married. The first name of her second boyfriend, and now husband, is also Dave. And not only is his surname the same last name that Shawn's previous boyfriend said he'd like to have, but her husband's name was actually changed to that name. When Dave's mother got divorced years before, she wanted a different last name. She changed her name and that of her two children to the name that Shawn's previous boyfriend happened to have liked.

The key ingredient for determining meaning in every mirror coincidence is identification of the charged complex. My neighbor, of course, is the subject and protagonist in this coincidence, and the charged psychological complex at work is a "true love" complex. When her first boyfriend no longer satisfied her true love ideal, she wanted a new, idealized true love, just as her boyfriend had wanted a new, idealized name. A name symbolizes, or is synonymous with, a person. She found a new true love, a new (literal and figurative) Dave. The new Dave even had a changed last name that was the same as the new name the old Dave desired. We can see that the coincidental circumstances mirror to a remarkable degree some of the components of my neighbor's charged complex.

What happened here? What caused this strange coincidence? Certainly, my neighbor had a lot of psychic energy focused on the desire for a new, ideal true love. It is also quite feasible that she might have unconsciously associated an idealized name, which the past lover desired, with an idealized lover she herself desired. However, we cannot go quite so far as to say her desire "caused" a model love with that name to materialize. The only thing we are able to state with confidence is that her very energized true love complex was an essential factor in the coincidence that mirrored it.

In *Synchronicity: The Bridge Between Matter and Mind,* F. David Peat presents some interesting suppositions about coincidence.[3] Using Jung's term for coincidence (*synchronicity*) he says, "as psychic patterns are on the point of reaching consciousness then synchronicities reach their peak; moreover, they generally disappear as the individual becomes consciously aware of a new alignment of forces within his or her personality" (Peat 1987, 27). This sounds nice, quite systematic. Unfortunately, it does not correlate well with reality.

It is simply the high level of excitation of a complex that is connected with the appearance of coincidences (synchronicities), and not whether someone is on the verge of becoming conscious of the complex. We previously noted that a complex, or its core component, may remain in the unconscious mind, totally hidden from awareness, although it is thoroughly charged with energy. However, using the above mirror coincidence as an example, it is irrelevant whether my neighbor's uncharacteristic behavior (when she hailed the man passing by on the beach) was a conscious attempt to find a new true love or a totally spontaneous gesture prompted by an unconscious urge. In either case, the coincidence is simply a function of her energized true love complex. In the case of my stepfather's stopped watch, he was already conscious of many of the factors that event, in association with retirement, symbolized. In "The Remote-Controlled Jet Liner" coincidence, which we'll look at shortly, we'll see that the distressed protagonist was always fully aware of her intense concerns.

Peat continues: "Synchronicities are therefore often associated with periods of transformation; for example, births, deaths, falling in love, psychotherapy, intense creative work, and even a change of profession. It is as if this internal restructuring produces external resonances or as if a burst of 'mental energy' is propagated

---

3. One problem I have with Peat's hypotheses is that, with one possible exception, the very few synchronicities (coincidences) he presents (which one would assume are the basis of his suppositions) are those that have been written about by other authors. There are virtually no first- or secondhand coincidences in his work.

outward into the physical world" (Peat 1987, 27). Here, Peat is closer to the truth. Coincidences do frequently occur in periods of transformation; again, the transformation of my stepfather's retirement accompanied by the coincidence of the stopped watch is such an occurrence.

However, the one key component is again the highly focused, high level of mental energy, which is likely to occur during those periods of transformation. This is true regardless of whether it comes in a burst or whether there is any "internal restructuring"; whether it is unconscious, "on the point of reaching consciousness," or primarily conscious. It is simply the factor of a complex's becoming highly charged with energy that is critical, regardless of on what level of consciousness the complex principally resides, and regardless of whether it is associated with a period of transformation. In "The Remote-Controlled Jet Liner" coincidence, we will look at a good example of a coincidence that does not involve a transformation of any kind and one in which the charged complex is entirely conscious.

CALLED FROM THE GRAVE?

In the first coincidence we discussed—that involving my stepfather's watch—the coincidental circumstances were simultaneous. In the previous example, the coincidence was simultaneous with, and a reflection of, my neighbor's excited true love complex. However, the coincidental circumstances, involving the names of her two true loves, were distant in both time and space. The definition of coincidence, "the concurrence of events or circumstances appropriate to one another or having significance in relation to one another," does not solely refer to a concurrence in time and space. When we say the events of a coincidence are concurrent, we mean concurrent in the sense of being "marked by accord, agreement, harmony, or similarity in effect or tendency." In other words, there is a common factor that causes the circumstances to be associated together, regardless of whether they occur together in time or space. The commonality may be in time, in space, in time and space, or in neither time nor space. An example of coincidental circumstances that are concurrent in space, but apparently not in time, is supplied by the following sequence of events.

The picturesque center of the town of Washington is situated on the crown of a hill in the Berkshire Mountains of Connecticut. A snow and ice storm was displaying nature's might there one winter day, when an elderly man drove by the cemetery in which his wife was buried. She had died only about a month prior. Just as he passed her gravesite, a large tree limb, laden with ice and buffeted by the wind, fell from an adjacent tree. It landed on his car, killing him. The events of this coincidence appear to be connected in space more than in time, in that the gentleman was next to the site where his wife was buried when he was killed.

Let's take a closer look at this coincidence. What provoked it? Some may claim that his wife "reached out from the grave to grab him." I don't think so. I mentioned that this coincidence is concurrent in space, but apparently not in time. Yet with what we know about a charged complex being associated with mirror coincidences, isn't it quite likely that there was a commonalty in time as well as in space?

We might surmise that, as the elderly man drove by the gravesite of his recently interred wife, his "lost love" complex was very charged. The gravesite reminded him of how lonely he was, how much he missed his wife, and how much he wished they were still together. Just then, a coincidence happened that mirrored his energized complex, effectively bringing them together beyond the physical realm. The only thing we can say with confidence is that a mirror coincidence emerged in which the circumstances were connected in space, and quite likely in time as well.

THE REMOTE-CONTROLLED JET LINER

In the introduction, it was noted that coincidences are, by definition, not a function of the law of cause and effect. Yet all the mirror coincidences we have looked at have been in association with highly energized psychological complexes. It is tempting to say that the complex somehow *causes* the coincidence, although there is no physical connection between the mental state and the coincidental event, and no known means of energy transfer from the one to the other. Yet the sequence of events naturally suggests to us that, although unknown, there are, in fact, forces at work that establish a cause-and-effect relationship between the aroused complex and the coincidental circumstance mirroring it.

It may be that we have more power in our own hands—or rather in our own hearts and minds—than we know. If that is the case, the problem is that it is both frequently an unknown power and one that we cannot manage or control. Yet sometimes, as in the following coincidence, the coincidental events almost make the protagonist appear superhuman.

A flight attendant for one of the country's largest airlines got off an airplane in Los Angeles. She was to remain there overnight in order to serve a flight back to the East Coast the next day. She was a commuter who lived near Washington, D.C., although based in New York. The flight attendant was newly hired and still on probation. This meant she could not yet use one of the extra "crew member seats" on a company airplane for personal travel, nor was she yet eligible to use employee travel passes to sit in vacant passenger seats. This made commuting between Washington and New York difficult.

The only option for free travel was through redemption of coupons "frequent flyer" customers are given and encouraged to award to flight attendants who provide exceptional service. If the flight attendant had friends or relations who happened to be members of the airline's frequent flyer program, she or he could also prevail upon them to pass along the coupons directly. As a result, this flight attendant had a substantial supply of coupons, obtained not only from passengers, but from friends and relations as well.

She kept all of these coupons in a large envelope, along with some other flight-attendant papers. On her flight to Los Angeles, she had taken a short break and sat down in the last row of seats in the airplane. Yes, I know, your experience has been that flight attendants never take a break, but are perpetually running up and down the aisle so that if you need something, like a pillow or an aspirin, they can be right there in an instant. In reality, once in a great while, one might take a break for, you know, just a minute or two.

Anyway, while on this short break, the flight attendant had put the large envelope containing the coupons in the seat-back pocket in front of her. No, the reason she put it there was not that she decided to read the latest issue of *Cosmopolitan* from cover to cover. You may be able to guess what happened next. When she got to her hotel in Los Angeles, she suddenly realized she had left the envelope with the flight coupons in the seat-back pocket.

She was beyond distraught. She envisioned being stuck in New York, separated from her home and husband for the four anguishing months remaining in her probationary period.

When she got to her room, still in a panic, she started making phone calls to various company agencies—crew scheduling, Los Angeles operations, system aircraft routing—to try to locate her precious envelope. Needless to say, her "fear-of-separation" complex was extremely energized. To her dismay, by the time she got through to someone who could provide her with accurate information, she found that the airplane was no longer in Los Angeles. So, if her envelope was, by good fortune, still in the seat-back pocket and not removed by the airplane cleaners, it was now probably about seven miles above the earth, on the way to some unknown destination. That was not very encouraging news, for this particular airline serves over 150 destinations in the United States alone, not to mention many foreign countries.

Eventually, she was able to determine the airplane's intended destination. This is when the frown on fortune's face changed to a smile. The airplane—almost as if she had willed it—was being flown to Washington, D.C., the airport nearest to her home.

The flight attendant called her husband, related what had happened, and told him the flight number and scheduled arrival time. She asked him to go the airport, meet the flight, and somehow find out if her envelope was still in the seat-back pocket. Next she called the airline back to let them know her husband would meet the flight. The company then sent a message to the pilots of the flight, letting them know the nature of this "national emergency."

After the flight had arrived and the jetway was hooked up, one of the flight attendants opened the passenger door to find an eager young man standing in front of her, wearing a look of concern.

The flight attendant smiled at him, said, "You must be looking for this," and handed him the treasure-laden envelope.

Let us review the sequence of events. A woman is in an intense state of distress. Her invaluable envelope is on the way to an unknown destination. Out of countless destinations, only one is a good one. That is where the envelope happens to be going. It seems as if some form of mind over matter is at work, the woman's intense desire appearing somehow to have arranged the airplane's destination.

Later in this chapter, in "The Mind as Magnet," we'll see that the assertion that the mind *does* have the power to influence events has been around for a long time. Here we may simply note that, again, we have a highly charged psychological complex, mirrored by a dramatic coincidence.

WHO'S GOT THE COMPLEX?

The sudden blooming of a coincidence in our hodgepodge gardens of existence is governed by few rules. We know that an energized psychological complex is perhaps the only requisite for the spontaneous emergence of a mirror coincidence, and yet even that rule may operate in unexpected fashion. One quirk of coincidence is that the person actually experiencing the coincidence may apparently be someone other than the person with the charged complex. This is illustrated by the following mirror coincidence involving one of Carl Jung's patients and the patient's wife.

The patient's neurosis had been resolved, and his treatment was coming to an end when he developed some minor physical symptoms that Jung concluded could possibly be an indication of heart disease. As a precautionary measure, Jung sent the patient to a specialist for an examination. Once the examination was concluded, the specialist gave the patient a note for Jung, stating he could find no cause for concern.

The patient's wife had previously related to Jung an unusual coincidence in relation to her mother and grandmother. On the occasion of each of their deaths, a number of birds had gathered outside the window of the room in which the person lay dying.

While walking home from the doctor's office with the specialist's note, which gave the patient a clean bill of health, the gentleman collapsed. When he was brought home, dying, his wife was already very upset. While her husband was away an entire flock of birds had alighted on the house. She, of course, recalled the earlier incidents when her grandmother and mother had died, and she feared a similar connection.

Although the wife may have had some mild concern about her husband's examination, he was only in his fifties, and the examination was merely a precaution. So she should not have been very anxious *prior* to the appearance of the birds. Once the symptoms of his heart attack became pronounced, the husband would logically be the one to experience the charged complex, the core component of which would be his fear of death. His wife would not be expected to have experienced a charged "death of spouse" complex until just after the coincidental circumstance—the arrival of the flock of birds—occurred.

In this case, the one who actually encountered the coincidence would seem not to be the person with the initial energized complex. One almost gets the impression that the foreboding flock of birds was a form of communication by the husband of his ordeal to his wife.

FLOODED, WITHIN AND WITHOUT

The following is an example of a mirror coincidence that reflects a highly charged *unconscious* complex. It is different from most of the coincidences we have examined in that it is not conclusive that a coincidence had occurred from a superficial look at the events. However, when all the events are viewed in conjunction with the psychological states of the participants, it is clear this is a classic mirror coincidence.

A woman was alone at night in a big house on the banks of a large river in southern New England. She suffered from a severe case of depression and was in a very agitated state as a consequence of the competition between highly charged, incompatible components of her psyche. Outside, the darkness was intensified by thick clouds that obscured the night sky and the heavy rain of a raging storm. The violent weather outside in the dark seemed to reflect her turbulent state within. In fact, the effects of the storm even penetrated the house, for the cellar was flooding, just as the woman's unconscious was flooded with potentially uncontrollable impulses. Into this scene entered a man, soaking wet, wild-eyed, and disheveled. He began knocking loudly on the door. He said he was lost. He wouldn't go away.

The woman called the police. When the police arrived, the man was nowhere to be found. After the police left, the man again appeared. This time he said he needed help. He said he was afraid he might hurt someone. The woman called the police a second time, engaging the man in conversation from an upstairs bedroom while keeping the police on the telephone until a patrol car returned to take the unfortunate soul into custody.

The police later called to relate that the man had escaped from a mental institution earlier that day. Apparently, he had walked approximately eight miles in extremely inclement weather, traversed a forest in encroaching darkness, and then swum a hundred yards across a swollen river. After he had surmounted this last obstacle, which happened to be next to the house in which the equally (though differently) distressed woman resided, he ended his journey, almost as if he had reached his goal.

In dream analysis—symbol analysis—the basement of a house symbolizes the unconscious. For Freud, it symbolizes the lower instinctual urges of the libido. Still, the flooded basement may have had no relationship to the woman's unconscious mind, flooded with conflicting impulses. Perhaps the stormy weather also had no relationship to the stormy psyche of the woman. The end of the flight of the fleeing mental patient at the woman's house, after such a determined effort to proceed, may similarly not conclusively confirm a coincidental connection. The man's agitated mental state, reflecting the woman's own confusion and distress, likewise is not conclusively coincidental. His return to the premises shortly after fleeing there from the police, and then remaining there until they returned, again is not in itself proof of a psychophysical connection between the events and the woman's mental state. Yet all these circumstances taken together strongly indicate a mirror coincidence has occurred.

In the coincidence "The Case of the Wayward Bicycles," we'll see that two closely related people may be gripped by essentially the same complex, which the coincidence reflects. Here, however, we see two people who are unrelated and unknown to each other, whose related complexes reflect similar states of confusion and anguish, and make their sudden association a central coincidental circumstance. The flight, the raging river, their agitated mental states, the storm, the flooded basement, their unexpected association, and the police are all either psychological or psychophysical components of the coincidence.

Earlier, we saw that, with her true love complex electrified, my neighbor seemed to draw to herself a love with the same name that her previous love wished he had. Here, it seems that the distressed woman in the house with the flooded basement on the dark and stormy night attracted another person, the mental patient, in a state of conflict and confusion that reflected her own.

THE MIND AS MAGNET

In the course of history, many individuals have asserted that we do have powers of attraction or repulsion. One such person was Goethe, the famous German poet and intellectual. He maintained that "we all have certain electric and magnetic powers within us, and ourselves exercise an attractive or repelling force" (Jung 1973, 33).

We have all heard that "opposites attract," usually in reference to relationships, particularly romantic relationships. It certainly is true of magnetic poles, but in regard to human beings, the statement is blatantly false. In the vast majority of cases, "like attracts like." The cases where apparent opposites form a close social or romantic relationship are relatively rare. That is why those relationships attract our attention. Furthermore, in the majority of those cases, the partners are merely apparent opposites. On closer examination, one would find that the personality projected by one of the partners masked contrary tendencies. Though powerful, these tendencies normally remain hidden, perhaps residing in the subconscious, and in that case, even hidden from the person possessing them.

Many of us know people who are unlucky in love. They seem always to fall into romantic relationships with someone who turns out to be manipulative, abusive, or unfaithful. We could just call it bad karma, but from a psychological perspective, there is an unperceived, perhaps unconscious side of the person who is attracted to (and attracts) these types of unproductive or destructive relationships.

A recent study of college students found that women who had been sexually abused earlier in life were over 200 percent more likely to be sexually abused in their college years than those women who had no previous history of abuse. How does one explain such a significant statistic?

Individuals, particularly children, who suffer such trauma very often experience strong feelings of guilt. Although they are victims, they subconsciously feel responsible for the abuse, feeling that the unjust treatment was somehow deserved. Their guilt, along with other painful aspects of these experiences, causes them to have negative feelings about themselves. Although these feelings, and frequently the actual incidents, may be repressed in the subconscious, they are a very potent part of the psyche. According to what has been noted about human psychology and about coincidence, such a negative complex tends to render the individual vulnerable to further negative and traumatic events that reflect the original.

Albertus Magnus, the teacher of St. Thomas Aquinas, embraced the views of an earlier, Islamic philosopher Avicenna, who wrote about the power of intense emotion. His words, written nearly a thousand years ago, are very interesting in the context of this subject and in regard to the general relationship between complex and coincidence:

> A certain power to alter things indwells in the human soul and subordinates the other things to her particularly when she is swept into a great excess of love or hate or the like. When therefore the soul of a man falls into a great

excess of any passion, it can be proved by experiment that it (the excess) binds things (magically) and alters them in the way it wants. . . . I found that the emotionality of the human soul is the chief cause of all these things, whether because, on account of her great emotion, she alters her bodily substance and the other things towards which she strives, or because, on account of her dignity, the other, lower things are subject to her, or because the appropriate hour or astrological situation or another power coincides with so inordinate an emotion, and we (in consequence) believe that what this power does is then done by the soul. . . . Whoever would learn the secret of doing and undoing these things must know that everyone can influence everything magically if he falls into a great excess . . . and he must do it at the hour when the excess befalls him. (Jung 1973, 32)

The last statement, "Whoever would learn the secret of doing and undoing these things must know that everyone can influence everything magically if he falls into a *great excess* [italics mine] . . . and he must do it at the hour when the excess befalls him," brings to mind the mirror coincidences we have been investigating. The "great excess" referred to is, of course, the highly energized or charged state of a complex.

A variant of this type of coincidence, in which an individual suffers great excess, is the coincidental connection between prayer and its results. Scientifically speaking, there is no cause-and-effect relationship between prayer and the events that satisfy its intent. Yet, when a prayer is answered, the psychological state is clearly connected in a meaningful manner to the psychophysical event that follows. Therefore, an answered prayer closely resembles the coincidences we have been discussing. We may perhaps categorize it as a distinct form of mirror coincidence.

There are innumerable instances, both recorded and unrecorded, of prayers being answered. Of course, many times prayers are not followed by attainment of the sought-for goals. According to the observation Albertus Magnus cites, it is the energy invested in the prayer—how fervently one prays—that is crucial to its success. This conclusion is reinforced by the relationship between a high level of psychic energy invested in a complex and the occurrence of a coincidence reflecting the complex. Furthermore, many religious authorities attest to the importance of this factor, advocating that one, in effect, be consumed by the prayer in order to have the prayer answered.

Our comprehension of the factors at play in coincidence allows for an interesting supposition about prayer: The degree to which a prayer is morally appropriate or righteous is not necessarily critical to the fulfillment of the prayer; rather, it is the intensity of the feeling invested in the prayer that may determine whether the objective of the prayer is attained. Certainly, many answered prayers are not lofty. It may just as well be a somewhat superficial personal triumph, such as victory in a sporting event or some material goal, that is prayed for and gained.

THE POWERFUL BUT IMPERFECT TOOL

A highly energized complex, like that found in intense prayer, provides an individual with a potential tool for enhancing his or her quality of life. However, it is an imperfect tool. Even when a complex is largely conscious, and we acknowledge its potential power to bring events into alignment with it, the results are far from sure. How many fervent prayers have not provided the desired outcome? There are too many unknowns to allow for confident expectation of goal attainment.

The statistician will argue that any increased probability of success, even if unrealized in the majority of cases, still over time provides a significant advantage over others competing for the same goals. This is the principle that allows the casinos in Las Vegas and Atlantic City to prosper. However, one must possess adequate resources to invest in the increased prospect of success. While casinos have significant financial resources to cover short-term failures, most individuals have only a limited reservoir of psychic energy at their disposal. If this energy is heavily invested in enterprises that prove to be unproductive, then after a period of time, the collapse of the system—the individual—may occur.

But what if positive results can be consistently anticipated? For the sake of argument, let's say an individual—through knowledge of astrological influences, mystical mantras, recondite rituals, and powerful prayer utilizing focused intense emotion—is frequently able to have desires materialized. Does this person profit? All too often, the answer is no.

Those who are empowered, whether physically, financially, or intellectually, too often use their resources in a manner that is, in the long term, unproductive to themselves as well as to others. Most of us don't necessarily know what is best for us, what is really most conducive to becoming happier, richer, human beings. Sometimes hardship is necessary to bring out the best in us. Sometimes defeat is necessary to force us to focus on more realistic or more enriching goals.

The irony of prayer is that what is prayed for and received not only may not be morally uplifting, it may actually turn out to be harmful to the individual seeking it. A couple may long to be able to buy their ideal home, only to find the pressures of mortgage, taxes, and maintenance unbearable. Sought-for career goals may turn out to be totally unrewarding. According to what we have learned about mirror coincidence, if a psychological complex is highly charged, such as in fervent prayer, you may indeed attain what you desire, even if it is harmful to you.

I have a good friend who had been living alone for some time and strongly desired the intimate companionship of a woman. He did not want a friendship with just any woman. He wanted a very attractive woman, but couldn't find one to suit him. His longing was so strong that, one day, he prayed with intensity that such a woman would come into his life.

The next day, my friend, who is an electrician, was up on a ladder at work when he heard a woman's voice from the sidewalk below. He looked down to see a pretty woman standing by the ladder. She asked him his name. A conversation followed. He asked her out. She said yes.

Soon they were involved in a full-blown relationship. But the relationship didn't go too well, to say the least. It was wild and crazy and destructive. My friend suffered a lot, and in hindsight, he wished he had never encountered the attractive woman who seemed to reflect his desire so well. He is alone now, and again he desires female companionship; but he is afraid to pray for help. Maybe he just needs to contemplate his prayer, his true desires, more thoroughly.

DREAMS THAT COME TRUE

I have drawn, and will continue to draw, parallels between dreams and coincidences. With that in mind, there is a particular type of mirror coincidence I would like to discuss. This is a coincidence in which someone has a dream, and then what was dreamed happens, thereby comprising a mirror coincidence. This is a relatively common type of mirror coincidence.

In fact, my wife, Wendy, recently had a dream that was mirrored by a coincidence. She dreamed she had unexpectedly run into a professional associate who had recently obtained a transfer in his work assignment, a transfer that she, too, hopes to be awarded. In the dream, she just asked him a few questions about his new situation. She mentioned the dream to me the following morning.

It was quite unlikely that she would see this person, at least not until sometime after she had obtained her own transfer. Yet a couple of days later, the very next time she was at work, she called to tell me that what she had dreamed actually happened. She had unexpectedly run into the person and asked him the same questions as in her dream. It wasn't until afterward that she realized the occurrence was just like her dream.

Charles Dickens related a similar circumstance. Dickens dreamed he was at a party when a woman in a red dress inadvertently backed into him. The woman turned around to excuse herself and volunteered that her name was Miss Aimes. The next day Dickens and a friend had an appointment to meet for a mutual endeavor. Dickens arrived first. When the friend got there, he was accompanied by a woman wearing a red dress. His friend said he wanted Dickens to meet someone. Dickens replied, "I presume it is not Miss Aimes." Yet that was precisely the woman's name.

Earlier, in the introduction, I mentioned that most dreams are the creative, dynamic expression of areas of the mind that are charged with energy. We also know that mirror coincidences are a manifestation of the same thing. Thus it makes perfect sense that what is expressed in a dream may also be reflected in a coincidence. What is less clear is the explanation of how in some of these coincidences, such as Wendy's, the coincidental circumstances almost exactly duplicate the particular details of the dream and not just the underlying meaning.

An interesting theory about the duplication of dream events in actual life has to do with those feelings people sometimes get of—as one baseball great expressed it—déjà vu all over again. We remember very few of our dreams, and even fewer with clarity. Studies in laboratory settings have confirmed that whenever a sleeping person is experiencing "rapid eye movement" (rem), which is easily recognizable beneath the closed eyelids, he or she is dreaming. From this, it has been experimentally determined that we all dream a significant portion of the time we are asleep. Since most people rarely remember dreams, it is quite possible that in many instances where there is a sense of déjà vu, we are actually experiencing a mirror coincidence in which the dream that the coincidental circumstances mirror is not recalled or only subliminally recalled.

One thing we may state with confidence is that coincidences that reflect dreams, like all mirror coincidences, are a function of an energized complex. About Dickens's coincidence not much can be said, since we don't know the circumstances surrounding it, nor can we discuss it with the participants. The only thing that might be pointed out in passing is that the color red is no doubt significant. Red frequently symbolizes passion or strong emotion, since it is associated with fire and with the blood; the skin becomes reddish when, under strong emotion (such as passion), the blood rushes to the surface.

With Wendy's coincidence, the charged area of the psyche is easily identified. She is very eager for the transfer that was the subject of the conversation in the dream and the conversation in the coincidence. It is not surprising that she dreamed about it and that it might be reflected in a mirror coincidence.

Commentating on this phenomenon of dreams mirrored by waking events, Jung's protégé Marie-Louise von Franz said:

> Jung observed that frequently a patient would dream of symbolic images which then in a strange way coincided with outer events. If one looked at the latter as if they were symbols, they had the same meaning as the dream images. . . . In such moments psyche and matter seem no longer to be separate entities but arrange themselves into an identical, meaningful symbolic situation. It looks at such times as if physical and psychic worlds are two facets of the same reality. This unitary reality Jung called the unus mundus (the one world). (von Franz 1992, 99)

This sounds like the observations made by the four diverse authorities in the introduction, regarding the ultimate similarity of the nature of reality in dreaming and waking states. It is not just in coincidences that reflect dreams that, as von Franz says, "psyche and matter seem no longer to be separate entities." In all mirror coincidences this is how the physical is rendered psychophysical. We have noted many parallels between dreams and coincidences, between dreams and the physical world of the waking state, and between the psyche and the physical world that reflects it in mirror coincidences. The difference between dreams and the waking state, and between matter and the constructions of the mind, appears to be more a difference of degree than a difference of type, as Jung's recognition of a "unitary reality," an *unus mundus*, apparently indicates.

THE CASE OF THE WAYWARD BICYCLES

As von Franz's observations suggest and Dickens's coincidence supports, dream-related mirror coincidences may be symbolic. We have also seen degrees of symbolism in some of the other mirror coincidences, such as that associated with a name or a watch stopping. Yet we have not investigated any coincidences that are highly symbolic. Therefore, let us conclude this discussion of mirror coincidences by looking at a couple of coincidences in which the events are almost totally symbolic.

The mirror coincidence that began this chapter incorporated a circumstance (retirement) and an instrument (wristwatch) that are familiar to people in civilized cultures all over the world. This made it easy to see the symbolic connection between the end of the working phase of life and a watch that stops working. Since everyone relates to a watch in more or less the same way, it is what may be termed a universal symbol. Most of our symbols fall into this category. Their meaning is intuitively grasped by nearly everyone, whether they can explain how they arrived at the meaning or not. That is why we find them so often in myths, literature, paintings, and even advertising. They evoke the same emotions, thoughts, and feelings in nearly everyone.

The following mirror coincidence incorporates a universal symbol whose meaning (unlike that of my stepfather's watch stopping) requires a little bit of detective work to determine. A few years ago, in the town where I live, a couple bought a new home. They were in the process of moving from a house in an adjacent community, which they had rented while looking for a home to purchase. Since the two homes were only a few miles apart, the couple did most of the moving themselves over a period of about a week.

One night during this transitional period, the husband's bicycle was stolen from behind the new home. This was in spite of the fact that the bike was out of sight behind the house and the property was secured by a five-foot-high chain-link fence and locked gate. At the other house, the one being vacated, there were also two bicycles that had not yet been moved. These bicycles, which were secured by a chain and lock, belonged to the wife and one of the couple's adult children. On the same night that the husband's bike was stolen from the new home, the chain was broken at the old home, and the wife's bicycle was also stolen. Only the wife's bicycle was stolen at the second location, although, once the chain securing the bicycles was broken, both bicycles were equally accessible, and, in fact, the other bicycle was considerably more valuable.

Although these two communities are in a relatively high-crime area, it is rare to have a secured bike stolen from a private residence. To have both the husband's and the wife's bicycles stolen from two different homes in two different towns on the same night seems somewhat surreal. The fact that a second, better bicycle was left untouched convincingly reinforces the conclusion that this coincidence is central to the husband and wife.

What does it mean? This is the fun part of coincidences, playing detective. When we encounter such an inexplicable juxtaposition of events and circumstances that we know a coincidence has occurred, we still are faced with the challenge of successfully analyzing the clues to its meaning. Fortunately, in the coincidence we are investigating, an object familiar to everyone is central to the coincidental events. The bicycles conform to our definition of a universal symbol.

What does a bicycle symbolize? In the introduction, I suggested there are a few simple, reliable rules that should be used to successfully analyze symbols. One of these is that *meaning is related to the most essential function or quality of the symbol*. Since a bicycle is a universal symbol, establishing its essential function or quality is relatively easy. This makes determining its symbolic significance easier.

What is the essential nature of a bicycle? A bicycle is a *vehicle*. We might go a little bit further in concluding it is a personal vehicle, in contrast to a public vehicle such as a bus, train, or plane.

A personal vehicle is generally operated by the individual and is done so more or less for his or her exclusive use. There is another type of vehicle that the individual uses to travel through life: our bodies and our personalities together constitute the vehicle that the soul, the enduring self, uses to travel from beginning to end of this life. In dreams and coincidences, personal vehicles such as a car or bicycle are spontaneous symbols for the individual self of this lifetime, this journey.

We're now aware that mirror coincidences reflect a complex that is charged with energy. Therefore, regardless of whether symbol analysis is used to determine the meaning of a particular coincidence, another factor must *always* be ascertained with mirror coincidences. What is going on in the lives of the participants? What complex is charged? Meaning stems from this. In coincidences with symbolic content, this will provide clues to the symbol's specific meaning in the context in which it is used and help verify or discredit our tentative appraisal of meaning. If our symbol analysis is supported by what is going on with the participant(s), that information will allow us to paint a more complete picture and be more precise in our analysis.

In the coincidence we are investigating, the couple's psychological state at the time the bicycles were stolen was dominated by distress concerning the welfare of one of their adult children, who was suffering from very severe emotional problems. In the past, this person had occasionally criticized the parenting and home environment provided by the parents. However, both of the couple's children had attained graduate degrees and respectable jobs, and they appeared to be functioning relatively well. Thus, the criticism had previously not been threatening to the parents.

No one is a perfect parent. This couple had grown up in Europe during the turbulent times of World War II. Those years had been difficult, and it was only natural that these difficulties might affect their early adult years of parenting. When the elder child quit work, dissolved a marriage, and was struggling to function in life, it was natural for the parents in this close-knit family to look back to their roles in the early child-rearing years. Whenever a child has personal problems, it is difficult for a parent not to experience feelings of guilt for real or imagined shortcomings.

This was the situation at the time of the stolen-bicycles coincidence (the psychophysical event reflected the psychological state). The parents were very distressed about the emotional health of their child and concerned about the role they may have had as parents to contribute to it. Knowledge about this situation—this charged complex—may help to determine meaning, and certainly should help verify it. With this in mind, let's take a closer look at the symbolic meaning of the bicycles.

In situations such as this one, when two objects mean generally the same thing, and one is used as a symbol instead of the other, there is a reason. The one used is somehow more appropriate than the other. Therefore, we need to ask, what distinguishes a bicycle from, say, a car, which is also a personal vehicle?

In the United States, from the age of sixteen on, we mostly likely use a car as a means of personal transportation. Prior to that age, we most likely use a bicycle. Therefore, the bicycle, which, as a vehicle, symbolizes the person, also represents something by its association with youth.

Youth is characterized by innocence and spontaneity; thus, it is logical to assume that the bicycle, the specific personal vehicle in the coincidence, symbolizes innocence. Another attribute of a bicycle in America is that, particularly for adults, it is a recreational vehicle. As such, it is associated with carefree, lighthearted, and healthy activities.

Thus far, our detective work has led us to deduce the bicycles symbolize innocence, perhaps coupled with a carefree, lighthearted outlook. This conclusion is also partially derived from our knowledge of the psychological state of the parents at the time of the coincidence. Just as the bicycles were stolen, the couple likewise had something else taken from them. They lost their innocence—their innocence as parents—and perhaps a certain lightheartedness and carefree attitude.

The stolen bikes symbolize the particular loss of innocence that dominated the psychological state of the couple at the time of the coincidence. Their loss of innocence in their role as parents is the charged complex that this mirror coincidence reflects.

The conclusions arrived at here are logical. They do not require psychic or significant intuitive abilities. A basic, straightforward analysis of the symbol's essential qualities, aided by awareness of the psychological complex that was charged in the individuals who encountered the coincidence, were all that was required.

CALIFORNIA AND CONNECTICUT CONNECTED

Sometimes, we encounter a coincidence that doesn't seem to present us with meaning or whose meaning appears too esoteric to grasp. The coincidence seems neither to mirror a charged complex nor provide us with direction.

About ten years ago, my mother, who lives near New Haven, Connecticut, decided she didn't need such a large refrigerator; it was time to replace it with smaller one. She placed an advertisement in the newspaper, offering the old refrigerator for sale. A young woman called, came to look at the refrigerator, and bought it. In the course of conversation, my mother was surprised to learn that the woman had recently moved to New Haven from Stockton, California. Mom happens to have a cousin, Roy, who lives in Stockton.

When my mother related this to her guest, she was even more surprised to find that the woman had been Roy's secretary at the bank in Stockton where Roy was vice president. What are the odds that a onetime employee and friend of my mother's cousin, in a town a whole continent away, would show up at Mom's house in response to an ad for a refrigerator for sale?

This sure looks like a valid coincidence, but what can its meaning possibly be? If I were one of the participants, if at least some meaning was not readily apparent, I would attempt to talk with others involved, looking for some similarity or some connection that may shed light on meaning. Certainly, it is important to see if there is anything at work that might serve as a component of a charged complex. The essential nature of potentially symbolic components should be contemplated in respect to these inquiries. If these efforts fail, the only thing we can do is store the coincidence away; meaning may be revealed at some point in the future.

A lot of people like to make things just for the fun of it. Sometimes it appears that some mysterious force has likewise created a coincidence just for fun. Regardless of whether meaning is found, the one thing immediately gained by such coincidences is a greater sense of the mystery and interconnectedness of all phenomena. One suspects that there are unseen and unknown forces playing hide-and-seek behind the mundane mechanics of life.

However, if we persevere in the search for meaning, it is likely that sooner or later it will be revealed to us. This is what happened to me in regard to my mother's coincidence. As we will see in chapter three, which focuses on the analysis of symbols, once I began to investigate the possible symbolic meanings of a refrigerator, and recalled some recent circumstances in my mother's life, the significance of the coincidence became quite clear.

Before we investigate the more frequent and more important directional coincidences, which can be very helpful in providing guidance to enrich our journey through life, it might be useful to review the significant points of this investigation of mirror coincidence. The one rule we can be sure of is that mirror coincidences are always associated with an area of heightened concern, a charged psychological complex. Particular concerns related to the coincidence are energized in those encountering all mirror coincidences. These concerns are not necessarily readily apparent to the casual observer, yet they are generally not difficult to identify by the one encountering the coincidence if he or she will take an open look within.

Occasionally, more in-depth detective work is necessary to uncover the charged complex and the meaning of the coincidence. As illustrated by the last two examples, this is often the case when the coincidental circumstances are symbolic. Yet in the chapter on symbols, we will find that the meaning of symbolic events can be unraveled without too much difficulty.

An important factor to note about mirror coincidences is that they generally *do not* provide us with significant guidance on how to conduct our lives more fruitfully and contentedly. One reason we need to be able to identify and analyze mirror coincidences is so we don't misinterpret their roles or confuse them with the more vital directional coincidences, which do provide us with individual guidance toward attaining enduring satisfaction.

The ability to identify mirror coincidences provides us with a greater capacity to understand the meaning of important events in our lives, whose significance would otherwise likely elude us. The essential contribution they provide is a better understanding of ourselves and the sometimes deeply hidden things that concern us, and a greater appreciation of the one vast, integrated entity we know as creation.

2 Directional Coincidence

THIS MORNING, as I strolled to the bay to watch the sunrise, I pondered off and on how to illumine the concept of directional coincidence, hoping for a ray of inspiration. Taoism, quantum physics, Hinduism, correspondence doctrine, and the concept of preestablished harmony are among various metaphysical perspectives that tend to substantiate the validity of directional coincidences. However, none of them appealed to me as the place from which to embark.

I didn't see the sun emerge from the ocean, nor its rays unobscured, until I was home again. Some low cumulus clouds hampered my view. The one circumstance that captured my attention was an encounter with nine golden macaws.

A golden macaw is a large, gorgeous, gregarious, parrot. Its breast and the underside of its large wings are the color of high-carat gold, while its back and the top of its wings are a blue that is bluer than the sky, almost indigo. They are, to me, a special treasure of the neighborhood. Their call is loud, frequent, and very distinctive: Whether flying or perched in a tree, their presence is usually announced by variations of *aawaaack*. I always call back.

I was walking homeward through a long, narrow, vacant lot, when I heard them in an adjacent Dade County pine. Of course, I had to stop and say hello. I was not surprised to encounter them, although I was at their number. I had never seen more than seven before. After Hurricane Andrew came huffing and puffing into town, they seemed to have disappeared. I was afraid it had blown them back toward their native habitat in Central and South America. But eventually I noticed one, then two or three at a time. Now, with at least nine in residence, my concern that there might not be enough for a viable breeding population may be put to rest.

The Jungians, mystics, and in general those who investigate symbols attend to the qualitative aspect of numbers—their symbolic significance. With such an unexpectedly large number of macaws, I contemplated the powerful symbolic qualities attributed to the number nine. However, none struck a chord of pronounced relatedness. I will still file it away, for now, as a pleasant little encounter, perhaps a coincidence of sorts.

When I returned home, still reflecting on an approach to directional coincidences, I opened a large book that I had recently received in the mail, an anthology entitled *Emanuel Swedenborg: A Continuing Vision*. Before me was an essay by Wilson Van Dusen: "A Mystic Looks at Swedenborg." Van Dusen, in a small book entitled *The Natural Depth in Man*, introduced me to Swedenborg many years ago. And as coincidence would have it, his essay had something to offer.

Van Dusen devotes quite a bit of his essay to discussing the attributes of a "mystical experience." He says a mystical experience is "characterized by direct knowing" (Van Dusen 1988, 216), an absence of doubt. This is certainly true of the most profound mystical experiences. Suddenly, there is a vision or a vital apprehension of some deeper aspect of reality, accompanied by a sure sense that what was perceived is absolutely true. But there are various levels of mystical experience, and an unshakable conviction in the revelatory nature of the experience is not requisite of all of them. In fact, *directional coincidences* may be, according to my conception, a type of mystical experience. So let us clarify what is meant by a mystical experience and a mystical perspective of reality.

A mystical experience is, to me, one in which the individual perceives, to some degree, the oneness of all of creation, the unity in diversity. One perceives that God is inherent in everything. The experience also fosters a sense of harmony and glorious mystery in the world about us. A mystical experience may occur when sitting on the back porch in the fading glow of a sunset, watching a couple of children playing with the dog on the lawn, while the last rays of the sun play with a distant cumulus cloud, which now and then spits fire. Then there comes the call of the whippoorwill, the cry of the loon, or an owl's haunting hello. Suddenly, there is a warm appreciation of the mystery, the harmony, and the oneness of it all, and a feeling of complete contentment. This is also a type of mystical experience.

A mystical perception is essentially one in which the individual grasps the full truth of the Judeo-Christian recognition that God is omniscient, omnipotent, and especially, omnipresent. Being omnipresent, of course, doesn't just mean that, when we kiss hello, or argue, or a child snitches a cookie, God is there watching. Omnipresent means contained in everything but confined by nothing. God is in the earth, the trees, the flowers, but also in the chair, the broom, the dirty dishes, an annoying fly, and most certainly in you and me. This feeling of oneness and harmony with God's presence in all things is the primary characteristic of a mystical experience.

God's omniscience is a total awareness in which no event or thing—not so much as a leaf in the breeze—escapes God's notice. And in God's omnipotence, everything is within his power.

So it is from this perspective—a sense of God's awareness, power, and presence, all about us—that directional coincidences are viewed, with one added ingredient. Van Dusen relates that his first mystical leanings surfaced when, in early adolescence, he would steal away to the roof of the family flat in San Francisco to witness the magic of the descent of evening upon the city. He thought he was alone in this type of reverie until he came upon a small treasure in a book store, a five-cent copy of Thomas Troward's *Edinburgh Lectures in Mental Science.* He found echoes of his own experience in Troward's words: "But because the universal personalness is the root of all individual personalities, it finds its highest expression in response to those who realize its personal nature" (Van Dusen 1988, 215). Beyond God's vast powers, it is his personal nature that is the crucial ingredient of directional coincidences. The guidance provided by directional coincidences is a product of God's personal love and concern for each and every one of us.

LIFE OR DEATH

The distinguishing characteristic of a directional coincidence is that it provides personal guidance in how to proceed toward realizing happiness and fruitfulness. That's the case for all but the most sensational directional coincidences, those in which either an activity is prevented or one is compelled to take a particular unanticipated action that ultimately turns out to be lifesaving.

Instead of guidance on *how* to proceed, such coincidences provide circumstances which *allow* one to proceed, rather than having life cut short. If the coincidental circumstances do not generally incorporate any additional guidance in how to enrich one's life, then it is not the type of coincidence that is the focus of this investigation. Here we are more interested in directional coincidences that provide instruction useful toward the ongoing fruitful conduct of our lives. Examples of their frequency, the way they appear when needed, their sometimes subtle nature, and their variety will perhaps be best illustrated in the section of this chapter on directional coincidences associated with the writing of this book.

Yet the more dramatic, life-saving coincidences, a few examples of which we'll touch upon now, should be included if for no other reason than simply to ensure that a complete picture of directional coincidence is presented. In addition, some of these coincidences go beyond the lifesaving function to indicate also appropriate ways to conduct the life that was saved.

One such coincidence, which was remarkable for the number of lives protected, was reported in *Life* magazine some years ago. One evening in a small town in Nebraska, fifteen people were to attend rehearsal for the church choir. Five minutes after practice was scheduled to start, the church was destroyed in an explosion. Fortunately, some of the members were not ready to leave for church on time: a car wouldn't start; a dress needed to be ironed; an interesting radio program was listened to until it concluded; a daughter had difficulty getting up from a nap when called by her mother. In fact, there were ten unconnected reasons that all fifteen members of the choir arrived after the explosion destroyed the church (Vaughan 1979, 167).

We should have no difficulty in classifying this divine intervention. Of course, one point being made about all directional coincidences, no matter how dramatic or subtle, is that they all are a product of divine invention and, to some degree, intervention.

In chapter one, it was noted that sometimes the events of a coincidence may be connected in neither space nor time, but may be concurrent or connected in the sense of "being in agreement, in harmony, or possessing similarity in effect or tendency." The following is such a case.

In the mid-1920s, when he was in his early teens, my father went to a dentist and donned a gas mask in order to be rendered unconscious. He didn't have to do this. His older brother did, because he needed some teeth removed, although he was terrified of the prospect. My father, being a pretty cocky kid, said there was nothing to it, and just to prove it, he'd go to the dentist with his brother and take gas first.

One winter day in Connecticut, close to thirty years later, my father and we four young children had just crested a long hill in our rather old car when he felt a pronounced pressure on his head, a ringing in his ears, and the need to take a big breath of air. He immediately recognized all the same symptoms that occurred just before he blacked out so many years before, when he volunteered to be the guinea pig for his brother at the dentist's office. He instantly knew we were suffering from carbon monoxide poisoning.

Most of us children were already asleep from the carbon monoxide when my father marshaled all his remaining awareness and strength to open his window, then bring the car to a stop and throw open the doors. He is convinced that because, by coincidence, he had experienced the same symptoms so many years before, he was able to avoid a potentially tragic accident. Perhaps the best proof that his insight is correct is the depth of his conviction in the coincidental connection between the two events.

A few moments ago, I mentioned that some of these directional coincidences in which a catastrophe is avoided are central to the purpose of this investigation. I suspect they are a greater number than we think. I am referring to those coincidences in which the action or circumstance that allows the tragedy to be eluded may itself provide additional direction—may present a lesson or other guidance toward fruitfully proceeding with the life that was saved.

In the first chapter, one of these types of directional coincidences in which disaster is dodged was briefly presented in the example involving Wendy's cousin. In order to hang out with other friends whom she unexpectedly encountered, she left a car and its occupants, who a short time later were involved in a fatal accident.

Let us say, just for the sake of argument, that these friends in their late teens occasionally indulged in activity involving illegal and unhealthy substances and that they were doing so on the night of the accident. In that case, leaving the vehicle, which was destroyed along with all its occupants, becomes a very dramatic statement to the one who left: that such activity is inappropriate, unhealthy, and potentially fatal. In other words, the coincidence would then both have saved her life and provided guidance on how to appropriately conduct it in the future.

A coincidence in which death was sidestepped and guidance was provided was told to Wendy by one of her friends in the aftermath of a recent airline accident. When this friend's father and mother were dating, they both worked for an airline. Her father was a pilot, and her mother was a flight attendant. Her father's cousin was throwing a big party in Las Vegas, to which her father wanted to bring her mother. However, her mother was scheduled to work that day.

Her father insisted on finding another flight attendant to take her place at work. It must have been true love, for he paid $100, a lot of money back then, to the flight attendant who replaced his beloved on the trip that interfered with their plans. It turned out to be money well spent, for the flight her mother was supposed to work crashed, killing all on board.

I think we can agree that beyond saving the woman's life, there was additional direction in this coincidence for the two of them.

Since it was her boyfriend's strong wish that she accompany him and his generosity that saved her life, it appears they were being directed to spend their lives together. They thought so, too. And once married, she had to give up flying, for in those days that airline required its flight attendants to be unmarried.

WHAT CONSTITUTES COINCIDENCE?

Sometimes, unusual circumstances occur together in such a manner that we suspect they constitute a coincidence, but there is still an element of doubt as to whether the events are really related in coincidental fashion. So, it may be a good idea to address this question: Beyond the definition of coincidence, what actually is, or is not, a coincidence?

If you go out to get the mail and happen to encounter your neighbor doing the same, no one would consider that much of a coincidence. On the other hand, if you bump into your neighbor in the appliance section of a department store, while shopping two towns away, that might be considered a minor coincidence. However, if you are showing off your expertise on the slopes of Jackson Hole, Wyoming, when an icy mogul gets the best of you, and the passing skier who retrieves an errant ski happens to be that same neighbor (who you didn't know skied)—now that is a coincidence. It is essentially a matter of degree—how unusual or unexpected is the situation?

What constitutes a coincidence? First, it must conform to the definition of coincidence. That is a given. Again, coincidence is defined as "the concurrence of events or circumstances appropriate to one another or having significance in relation to one another but between which there is no causal connection." This definition has been adequately discussed in the introduction and in chapter one, so it should not need further amplification here.

Yet we are still left with the question of what exactly constitutes a coincidence. In my view, any experience that is very unusual and unexpected should be considered a potential coincidence. If something could have happened hundreds or thousands of times before, but did not, and then on one particular occasion, it does happen, it should be treated as a potential coincidence. The reason I take this approach is that, in over a quarter of a century of investigating the phenomenon, I have found it to be valid and fruitful.

The word *potential* is very important. An attention-getting, unusual, and unexpected event may not be treated as an actual coincidence unless it can be classified as a psychophysical event—an event that is in some way related to me or to the situations in which I am involved. If I am confronted with a very unusual, unexpected circumstance, I look to see if it might have significance in relation to some situation in my life, recognizing that this significance may have been either directly or symbolically expressed.

Let us look at a hypothetical case. After you complete a power walk along the beach, you decide to dive into the ocean to cool off. When you surface, you experience an instant of dread and fear as two large dorsal fins break the surface ten yards away. A second later, you are relieved, then excited, to realize it is a pair of dolphins rather than sharks.

You notice they are feeding on a school of fish, and, entranced with their coordinated actions, you watch as they work the fish. After some minutes, they seem to have satisfied their appetites, for they abandon the fish. Still, they remain close by for a while, seeming to play with each other for your entertainment, for twice, when they surface, you have direct eye contact with them. You have lived near the ocean all your life and frequently visit the beach, but this is the first time you have ever seen a dolphin, much less two.

It is so unusual that you think it may have some meaning—it might be a coincidence. The thing that most strikes you about the dolphins is how well they work together and that they seem to be having fun together. You know that, like yourself, dolphins are mammals. You stop to ponder whether there is anything going on in your life right now to which they might relate.

Your best friend recently invited you to join in a minor business venture. In fact, on the way to the beach, you had been pondering the issue. While in school, you and another friend had started a small business; but it did not work out well, and the friendship was never the same afterward. The situation is different with your best friend, whom you trust and with whom you have such good rapport. Nevertheless, when the proposal for the business venture was made, you felt a strong sense of anxiety and evaded the issue.

It was somewhat similar to the feeling of silent panic you experienced when the two dorsal fins first appeared above the surface. But they turned out to belong to dolphins, not sharks—and dolphins that worked together as well as they played together. You tentatively conclude that these two dolphins might represent you and your best friend. And your unexpected encounter with them for the first time in your life may have been a directional coincidence, encouraging you to accept your friend's business offer. Therefore, you give that proposal more open and serious consideration than you otherwise would have.

This is an example of how examining current circumstances can help indicate whether situations are coincidental. The next step for you would be to investigate the business proposal more fully, instead of simply rejecting it because of your previous experience.

There is a very practical reason for recognizing that unusual and unexpected circumstances may be components of a coincidence. The meaning conveyed by coincidences is frequently useful in guiding our activities and personal development. Unusual and unexpected situations are treated as potential coincidences because it is the intelligent thing to do. The more intelligent behavior is to treat something as potentially meaningful—which may be later discarded if meaning cannot be established—rather than dismissing it in the first place as not worthy of consideration.

The openness to the possibility that any unusual and unexpected event may be a component of a coincidence is allowable only if we don't overestimate perceived meaning. If every unusual or mysterious encounter prompted a radical reaction, then it would be better to treat nothing as meaningful except those things that are obvious products of a physically apparent cause-and-effect relationship. Potential meaning of a probable coincidence is always weighed with other known factors in our lives. And even if other circumstances support the likely meaning of an apparent coincidence, the general rule in acting upon the meaning is to use caution.

COINCIDENCE AND ROMANCE

The quality and general characteristics of a marriage or a close romantic relationship are very important influences on our progress along the path of life. They may enhance happiness and nurture growth, or they may retard development, stifle creativity, and foster misery. The question of whether a relationship should be entered into with a specific person is an important one. There are also many options of how these romantic unions, if entered into, will continue—whether they will be fruitful and enriching, or negative and destructive. Finally, one invests a lot of psychic energy in a relationship, and even when not involved in a relationship, if one is longed for. For all these reasons, romance is a very fertile ground for the sprouting of coincidences.

We have already witnessed this with the mirror coincidences discussed in chapter one, in which many of the coincidences we investigated involved romance in one way or another. Actually, this is quite understandable when we consider that romance is usually charged with the psychic energy that precipitates mirror coincidences.

For many of the reasons noted above, romance is also a fertile ground for directional coincidences. Like the coincidence in which a future husband's desire for his beloved's company saved her from being a victim in a terrible accident, the following coincidences (although not in quite as spectacular a fashion) illustrate how directional coincidences may come into play in romance.

THE WINNING COMBINATION

A friend of mine, Jerry, who does volunteer spiritual development work in prisons throughout the country, came to Miami for that purpose. He stayed in my home for the few days that he was in town. On the first evening, I enquired if any dramatic coincidences ever happen in his life. He responded enthusiastically that he just had a good one.

His girlfriend had a dream of a landscape in which four very large luminous numbers rose up out of the earth. The glowing numbers that emerged from the ground were 1440. Jerry lives in the Baltimore area, and he concluded that those prominently displayed numbers might be good ones to play in the Maryland daily lottery. He bought two tickets, one for himself and one for his girlfriend, for the numbers 1440. That day, the winning number was not 1440, but the exact total of the two tickets added together: 2880.

I suggested that, since the winning number was formed by adding his and his girlfriend's numbers together, the coincidence might be saying that they should get married, that doing so would form a winning combination. He said that his girlfriend suggested the same thing. The fact that the winning number was the total of their two identical numbers, rather than two different numbers, might be interpreted as an additional positive sign, symbolically saying that they were alike and compatible.

I also pointed out to Jerry that there was another coincidence that provided additional evidence for the marriage interpretation of his coincidence. He happened to be relating his coincidence to me in my home the day before my own wedding to Wendy.

This coincidence is a good example of a directional coincidence in which the meaning appears clear. There is only one problem with this interpretation, one qualifier. Although I didn't realize it at the time, there is a possibility Jerry's coincidence could have been a mirror coincidence. If Jerry's girlfriend had a very strong desire to get married, the coincidence might have reflected the charged marriage complex, rather than having been purely directional in nature. Still, the fact that the coincidence did not mirror the dream content, but rather continued to unfold the drama, perhaps suggests that it was more directional than mirror in type.

Nevertheless, this does illustrate the danger of offering advice or an interpretation when one's knowledge is limited. If I had known then what I now know, I would have asked Jerry what his girlfriend's attitude was prior to the dream. Did she previously advocate marriage, and if so, how strongly? Regardless of his girlfriend's outward attitude, I would have cautioned that, although it does appear to be a genuine directional coincidence, it is possible that the coincidence is merely a symbolic reflection of her strong desire for marriage, either acknowledged or hidden.

Kahlil Gibran to the Rescue

The following is a coincidence involving marriage in which there can be no doubt about the coincidence's directional nature. A couple in San Francisco who were dating were apprehensive about tying the knot, for it would be the second marriage for both. One evening, a book that had hitherto remained unread on the shelf beckoned the man to read it. It was entitled *The Nature of Love*, by Kahlil Gibran. The gentleman was struck by some passages that seemed to be meant for his lover and him. He telephoned his sweetheart to read a passage to her. When he finished, she excitedly responded that she was holding the same book and had just finished underlining the same passage. Since they had never previously even mentioned the book to each other, this coincidence served to dispel most of their fears about marriage.

During their wedding ceremony, the minister read the particular passage from Kahlil Gibran that they had earlier excitedly shared over the phone. The groom winked at the bride, thinking it was her doing. The bride squeezed the groom's hand and said, "Thank you, honey," thinking he had arranged it. Later, they discovered that neither of them had talked with the minister about using that passage (Vaughan 1979, 141-2). If there were any residual doubts before the ceremony, with this additional coincidence, they were now thoroughly banished.

These last two directional coincidences have something in common beyond involving romantic relationships. They both also incorporate coincidences that are followed, at a later date, by additional coincidental circumstances that reinforce the original coincidence. In Jerry's case, the day and place that he related the coincidence was coincidentally the day before I was to get married and in the place where wedding festivities would be taking place. With the couple inspired by Kahlil Gibran, the added coincidence was even more dramatic, with the minister reading the exact passage that had stimulated their wedding plans.

This type of pattern happens fairly frequently with coincidences. A coincidence will be followed by one or more other sets of circumstances that are coincidental to the initial coincidence. Clearly, in such situations, we can only assume the additional events provide greater emphasis on the appropriateness of the guidance we have received.

That is somewhat different from situations in which there will be a number of different coincidences—some dealing with the same or related topics—occurring in short succession. In those cases, it is as if it is the season for the blooming of coincidence.

I have a key lime tree in my yard. There always seems to be a few fruit on it. But a couple of times a year, the tree will be adorned with an abundance of the small, round, yellow fruit. Directional coincidences are like that. There are seasons when they are most abundant. The season is largely dependent upon the individual and his or her personal openness and receptivity to guidance. It is influenced also by whether there are one or more areas in the person's life that are in a state of flux or transition, in other words, areas in which there are options in courses of action, resulting in more opportunity and necessity to respond to guidance. Finally, as with mirror coincidences, the season may be influenced by whether there are particular areas of the psyche that are invested with energy, which a directional coincidence may relate to.

Better Locked Out

As we know, romance, or the lack of it, can arouse the focus of a high level of tension or psychological energy. Furthermore, an important romantic relationship may play a vital role toward stimulating, retarding, or defining the nature of an individual's development. This, coupled with the potent symbol of one's own automobile as an extension or representation of the individual, is a fertile combination for coincidences. A friend of mine encountered such a directional coincidence, which at the time left him with the impression that the impossible had happened.

This man was totally caught up with a woman who was finding life too conflicting to be dealt with effectively. She became involved with another man whom my friend was convinced would just cause more problems and confusion for her. He decided to attempt to express his concerns to her in person, although this would entail driving some distance.

As he left home, he saw that he needed gas, so he stopped to get some cash from an ATM. Since it was a hot summer day, when he got to the nearby cash machine, he just got out of his car and slammed the door, leaving the car running with the air conditioning at maximum cold.

When he returned to the car with the money in hand, he could not open the door. It was obviously locked, although that seemed impossible. In the three years that he had the car, he had come to accept the minor inconvenience that the only way the driver's side door could be locked when leaving the car was with the ignition key. Once the door was opened, it could not be locked using the lock on the interior of the door.

Now, all of a sudden, the door was locked from the outside although the key was still in the ignition. Not only was the key in the ignition, but the car also was running, the air conditioning was on max, and the gas gauge was on empty. The car tended to overheat in stop-and-go traffic when the air conditioning was on high. He wondered what would happen first: Would the car stall from overheating, or stall from running out of gas? In either case, he realized the battery would be discharged because the air-conditioning was running at full blast.

In the midst of his panic, it did occur to him that maybe the weird circumstance of being locked out of his car in such an inexplicable manner was a sign that he should not go on his rescue mission. Nevertheless, when he finally found someone who had a tool that could be used to unlock the door, he did go forward with his mission. Of course, it turned out to be fruitless, and he later realized that indeed it was fortunate his mission was futile. Yet, when he was first provided with the directional coincidence of the inexplicably locked door, he was not receptive enough to respond to it.

Afterward, he was still mystified by the locked door, until I informed him that the driver's door of that make of car could be locked by pulling the interior door handle out, while the other hand simultaneously pushed the locking mechanism in front of it to the locked position. Without knowing he had done it, that one time, he must have inadvertently nudged the lock forward with his knee or opposite hand while the handle was pulled out.

And The Music Won't Play

I have encountered similar directional coincidences involving a budding romance and my car. One of note occurred on the island of Manhattan. I used to work near Manhattan, and for years regularly drove there to take tai chi chuan classes three times a week, and later, to attend graduate school as much as five days a week. Manhattan was then considered by many to be a pretty wild jungle, with an abundance of dangerous predators. Yet in all that time, neither I nor my car suffered at the hands of muggers or thieves.

This is not to deny that occasionally I would become somewhat wide-eyed with a mild sense of alarm. One such incident happened during my daily traverse of 125th Street in Harlem, en route to the Triboro Bridge. I was stopped at a red light on a warm spring day with both front windows rolled down, when I suddenly became very aware that the occupants of the cars on either side of me were angrily yelling at each other through my open windows—with me, so to speak, in the line of fire. I wondered which would come first, a green light or the muzzle of a gun? Of course, it was a green light. New York is really no different from any other city, except that the people are more direct.

My Manhattan directional coincidence occurred on a first date. A visit to a small park to relish the tender leaves and fragile blossoms of early spring preceded an intimate dinner in a cozy restaurant in Greenwich Village. When we returned to my car, I was dismayed to note that its right rear window had been smashed. My tape deck, which had been out of sight under the driver's seat, was stolen, as were my tapes.

I had removed the tape deck so a would-be thief would think it was either in my possession or in the trunk of the car. To me it seemed strange and illogical that someone would risk breaking into the car when the object of their break-in appeared to be absent.

Later, during my drive home, I contemplated whether there might be hidden meaning in the evening's events. I was well aware that, in dreams and coincidences, one's vehicle often symbolizes the individual. Damage to my car could symbolize and foreshadow physical or psychological damage to myself. Furthermore, the theft of the music and the tape deck could be interpreted as symbolizing the loss of not only some sense of enjoyment (the music), but also loss of the capacity (the tape deck) for enjoyment.

The next day, in response to a friend's question, I said I did not think I would pursue the relationship, that I did not feel that the chemistry was there. This was true, but I was also apprehensive about the potential symbolic significance of the coincidence that, on our first date, my car, for the first time, was broken into.

Nevertheless, perhaps because my desire for a close relationship was strong—or because it was after all just a coincidence—I eventually disregarded my more intuitive judgment and became heavily involved. As you must surmise, the symbolic meaning of this coincidence proved painfully correct. It was quite some time after the relationship was over before I had the psychological capacity to *play the music*—to fully enjoy myself in a lighthearted way.

Saved by the What?

It is difficult to follow the guidance of directional coincidences if we have only an intuitive sense of meaning, without possessing either support for their truths from other related circumstances or empirical knowledge of how they function derived from analysis of past coincidences. As my response above reveals, even when someone has a relatively high level of confidence in the meaning of a coincidence, which is further bolstered by gut feelings, it is of no benefit if one succumbs to needs and desires that patience and discipline might allow to be more appropriately satisfied elsewhere.

On the other hand, it is easy to comply with the instruction of a coincidence if it is in agreement with both intuition and desire. And it is easiest, as the next coincidence illustrates, if in addition it comes at just the right moment to provide freedom from a potential web of entanglement. I had a friend who was attractive, intelligent, creative, considerate, and attempting to cope with the fallout of a sudden, unforeseen divorce. I appreciated her creativity and enjoyed her company but felt it unwise to allow the friendship to spill over into romance. Yet early one evening, I was disconcerted to note that somehow we had arrived in my bedroom, on my bed, engaged in light physical contact.

Thinking it was inappropriate, I had little desire for actions to progress in the direction they were obviously headed. On the other hand, I did not want to be the bearer of another blow to my friend's self-esteem, so I felt trapped and unable to extricate us gracefully from this tricky situation. Just then, from a wall that we were not in contact with, a large, framed, Japanese wood block print fell tumbling onto the bed for no apparent reason. I immediately got up to put it in a safe place. And since both of us were sensitive to such unforeseen happenings, it was relatively easy to exit to a safer environment.

This coincidence may have been as much mirror as directional in that it provided the escape I hoped for. Yet it was certainly directional in that it dramatically impeded an impending course of action that was unwise.

Eldorado, the City of Riches

A more recent and perhaps most important directional coincidence providing guidance on a romantic or potentially romantic relationship was the one that pointed to the potential of the relationship Wendy and I share, and underscored the separate things required of each of us to ensure that potential would be achieved. The root of the coincidence was planted just on the other side of the Rio Grande, in Nuevo Laredo, Mexico. It bloomed in Atlantic Beach, New York, on the south shore of Long Island. And the fruit of it we enjoy here in Miami. It was, therefore, one of those coincidences in which the coincidental events shared a sameness of neither space nor time. A name was, in this case, that which formed the coincidental connection.

We had an opportunity to spend a couple of days in San Antonio, Texas. While there, we decided to take a drive down south of the border to Nuevo Laredo for sightseeing and dinner. In Nuevo Laredo, we looked for a place called the Cadillac Restaurant, which has long been popular with the gringos. We eventually found it, although the name had been changed (apparently when taken over by the son of the original owner) from the Cadillac to the Eldorado Restaurant. While there, we happened to get into an intense disagreement, which resulted in a premature departure and a drive back to San Antonio during which not a word was spoken.

The flames of high emotion ignited that evening gradually subsided to smolder barely noticed, although sometimes fanned to intensity by a sudden gust of discord. A week later, I was looking for a place for us to rent on the south shore of Long Island, for we were both working in New York at that time. One ad in a local paper offered two places in an area we liked. When the realtor took me to the first bungalow, I was alarmed to find it was on Eldorado Street.

In chapter one, when we discussed a hypothetical "intense love/ painful separation" complex and witnessed how previously neutral things could come to symbolize the core elements of a complex, we also saw how they may additionally come into play in coincidences. I suspected this was happening here, with Eldorado Street's being symbolic of the situation that surfaced at the Eldorado Restaurant. The negative, anxious feelings associated with the incident at the Eldorado Restaurant made me quite uncomfortable, so I was wary of living in a house that formed a coincidental connection with that incident by being on a street of the same name.

I had little doubt in my mind that there was a coincidental connection. To my recollection, prior to the Eldorado Restaurant, I had never previously encountered anything named Eldorado, although I was aware that it was the name of a model of Cadillac automobile, and I vaguely recalled something about a legendary city of gold named *El Dorado* in South America. Now, first to experience a heightened situation in a restaurant of that name and then, shortly afterward, to find a residence (which was too good to pass up) on a street of the same name seemed to be an obvious coincidence. The intensely emotional circumstance that surfaced in the Eldorado Restaurant was likely the psychological nucleus to which the psychophysical events of the coincidence were related.

The fact that the cottage was so perfect for us both complicated and substantiated matters. The bungalow on Eldorado Street was not only much better than the other house the realtor showed me, but was by far the most charming house I had seen or could hope to find in our price range. Furthermore, it was less than a block from the beach and less than fifteen minutes from work.

Wendy's work would keep her out of town for close to two weeks—by coincidence until the date the house was available—thus, after some hesitation, I decided we could not pass it up. I had a sense that we were supposed to live there—were being directed to live there—but I did not yet know why, and I was worried because of the incident at the Eldorado.

Gradually, my fears subsided as I grew to understand the true meaning of the beautiful bungalow, ideally situated on Eldorado Street. It symbolized the beauty and appropriateness of our domestic union, with the one important caution. We each needed to ensure that the separate issues that sparked our discord at the Eldorado did not threaten our new El Dorado—our place of riches—whether there on Eldorado Street or wherever it might be.

This we were able to accomplish, it seemed, simply as a result of making the commitment to do so. And it was there on Eldorado Street that we decided to get married. It was there, too, that I decided to take a year or so off from my career to write the book I had first begun a couple of years earlier, but could not find the resources of time and energy to proceed with in earnest while working full-time.

In retrospect, because of our commitment and efforts while on Eldorado Street, it was there that our El Dorado bloomed and elsewhere later brought forth fruit. Our haven of wealth, abundance, and opportunity, although not in South America, is now in our own home in the city farthest south in America, and at this point is not a material wealth, but the far more valuable treasures we discover daily in our lives together.

These examples should have provided you with the tentative realization that, at least in the important realm of romance, directional coincidences are not an anomaly. If you are not aware of coincidences occurring in this area in your past to provide guidance, I hope you will be alert to their flowering in future situations. Even if you are involved in a romance that is now an institution (as I am), there are many opportunities for directional coincidences to point the way to a richer life together.

ALONG THE PATH

One reason for choosing the coincidences used in this section, and those in the next section on coincidences associated with writing this book, is that the focus of this investigation is not the really dramatic or spectacular coincidences that we hear about now and then, or once in a great while encounter ourselves. The goal is to pass along some practical knowledge about the sometimes subtle directional coincidences that regularly appear in our erratic voyages, so we can use them to help navigate the tricky shoals of life in order to arrive on the shores of fulfillment and contentment. The coincidences we will be looking at are a small sampling of the many that continue to provide guidance toward the fruitful conduct of my own life.

Two Flags Equal One Sun

The first directional coincidence I can remember happened in Korea, over twenty-five years ago. It was not a really spectacular coincidence, but it had its share of drama. As with all directional coincidences, its meaning is what is important. It both pointed the direction the rest of my life was to take and revealed the requisites for its fruitfulness.

When I got out of college, the Vietnam War was going on hot and heavy. Most of my classmates either went to graduate school or into the military. I became a pilot in the Air Force.

I was on a three-year tour of duty to the Far East when the coincidence occurred. I spent a couple of weeks in Vietnam flying out of Cam Rahn Bay Air Base, on the now-serene shores of the South China Sea, followed by a short stay at home base near Tokyo, Japan, and then a couple of weeks at Suwon Air Base, which is about twenty miles south of Seoul, Korea. Then I would go back to Japan for a short while on the way to Vietnam.

I was an aircraft commander on a four-engine C-130, which carried close to two dozen crew members. C-130s were designed to carry cargo and troops and to drop either one, if necessary, from the air. They were primarily used as "trash haulers" in Vietnam, resupplying the sometimes besieged army in places like Pleiku, Phan-Rang, and Hue. But my aircraft had been modified to carry some very sophisticated equipment, and most of my crew were language specialists whose function was to eavesdrop. Our mission was reconnaissance, spying on the hostile forces.

There are a few things I remember most about Vietnam: the beautiful sunrises out over the South China Sea, punctuated by a few puffy altocumulus clouds; the incongruity of guys raising two fingers in the peace sign, while draped over the large machine guns mounted in the open "barn doors" of helicopters, as they passed close overhead those of us lounging on the beach; two magnificent waterfalls that I would always admire when flying up the Mekong River, which fell off a vast, very high plateau on the border of Laos and Thailand; and finding Carl Jung's *Man and His Symbols* in the base library at Cam Rahn Bay, which became my bible as I learned more about symbols in dreams, which later led to recognition of symbols in life.

We actually had closer calls in the missions we flew from Korea than those in Vietnam. In Vietnam, I felt as if I were watching a movie of the war, but from inside the movie. Until you got shot down, you felt a surreal sense of detachment, encapsulated above in your air-conditioned airplane.

The North Koreans were pretty aggressive then, and the Chinese too. Both of them used to send up fighter aircraft to try to shoot us out of the sky. In fact, the North Koreans shot down a Navy airplane conducting the same mission we flew, and President Nixon did not do a thing about it, although the airplane was over international waters. I guess he figured one war at a time was enough. The United Soviet Socialist Republic (as it was called then) was the only one we did not have much trouble with in that part of the world. We were issued a Nikon camera so we could take pictures of the Soviet migs when they flew alongside us.

My coincidence in Korea stemmed from a couple of visits to an ancient Buddhist monastery, which was just a bike ride from the air base. The first time I went there, I met a monk who had been a translator in the Korean War and thus spoke excellent English. We developed an immediate rapport. Consequently, the venerable monk who headed the monastery invited me to join their coterie for dinner. The meal was simple but fascinating with its precise rituals. Afterward, I was invited to visit again and stay the night, so I could participate in the evening and morning meditation and worship.

The main hall must have been saturated with the vibratory vestiges of a thousand years of meditation, for, on my return visit, my meditation, in which hours passed as minutes, was very deep and profound. Except for the patriarch, we all slept on straw mats in the main hall. I was awakened at about four o'clock by the haunting sounds of a wooden, hand-held drum. It was beaten in a cadence that gradually alternated between slow and very fast, while the monk carrying it walked around the perimeter of the monastery to purify the grounds. After washing, we went to the temple where I parroted a standing chant interspersed with many bows before Buddha. Meditation was followed by morning chores, which is when I took my leave.

I attempted to reciprocate for the kindnesses extended to me at the Buddhist monastery by inviting my friend, the monk, to dinner at the officer's club on the air base. I met him at the entrance to the base, where he presented me with some scrolls of rice paper upon which he had printed Buddhist scriptures from ancient wood block carvings. Our meal was quite natural and pleasant, although at the same time it seemed alien, unexpected, and special to be dining with a Buddhist monk at an American officer's club on a Korean air base, eating Western food.

As I escorted my friend off the air base, I pleasantly reflected on the uncommon portrait the two of us presented: the oriental in his white Buddhist robes beside the occidental in his Western civilian outfit, walking and talking in easy rapport. I felt very fortunate to have this association—to have been allowed to enter and participate in the mysterious world of the Buddhist monastery, the root of Eastern culture.

Approaching the main gate, we suddenly heard the resounding notes of the host anthem issuing from loudspeakers throughout the base. Directly before us, previously unnoticed, the stately flags of Korea and the United States were about to be lowered by the color guard below. No matter what he or she was doing, everyone all over the base stopped and was still, to show respect to the two nations whose flags were lowered in this daily ceremony.

We, too, stood still, while gazing at the flags that dominated the immediate landscape. Slightly above and directly between them, the sun hung huge and red above rugged, low mountains. The two apparent opposites, he and I, East and West, were reflected there before us, in the two flags illumined by the setting sun.

The Korean flag, which was lowered first, reiterated the union of opposites. For in its center was depicted the round diagram of the balanced interaction of the opposing yin and yang forces, whose interplay is seen in East Asia as the basis of all phenomena. After the United States' flag was met by the outstretched hands below and the strains of the American anthem were coming to a close, only the round red sun remained, unblemished, where the flags had been.

I sensed there was something very special about the uncommon symmetry of that scene. It was no mere accident that what was unfolding in my life was mirrored so well in the drama of the landscape we had just been a part of. I felt it was a graphic sign conveying the correctness of the paths I was pursuing.

In the three years or so that I spent in the Far East, there was first a meeting and then a marriage of the East and West within myself, a merging of what the East and the West characterize and symbolize. This union became the focal point of my life, the hub about which the rest has revolved. This coincidence both sanctioned this approach to life and learning and pointed the way the rest of my life would unfold.

The West is characterized by a mind that is rational, conscious, surface, pragmatic, technical, and masculine, which for me was represented by the role of officer and combat crew commander, flying technical, precise, sensitive missions. The East represents the fertile, unconscious, intuitive, romantic, deep, feeling, feminine mind, which is characterized by the use of meditation and analysis of the symbolic realm of dreams to explore the fertile depths of the unconscious, the love of nature and mystery, and the investigation of the underpinnings of the Eastern perspective on life via reading and direct exploration of the culture.

The round red sun, which remained at the end of this brief drama, points to the product that is to be born of this union of opposites. For the sun here symbolizes sound, symmetrical, undivided wholeness. It is also reminiscent of the soul at the root and core of our being as well as the oneness of all creation.

The rich, red color of the sun symbolizes the vibrant vitality of the state achieved by the balanced cultivation of both mindsets: East and West, feminine and masculine. The color red may also reinforce the soul aspect of the unblemished round sphere. It brings to mind the blood, which, as is underscored in the Christian sacrament of communion, may symbolize the vital spiritual ingredient without which life is impossible.

In looking back, I can see that, as my life unfolded, this same theme—the correctness of developing the unconscious, intuitive, receptive, feeling, feminine side of the mind to complement the natural posture of the Western male—has been presented to me many times. And the lessons have not been in vain. The balanced nurture of both natures has become in me an essential trait.

Carl Jung and his associates, in *Man and His Symbols*, also stressed the importance of this task. The female side of the male he called *anima*, and the male side of the female was termed *animus*. Jung stressed that each sex, in order to be well-rounded, whole, and healthy, and to realize its fullest potential, needed to develop the latent strengths of the opposite sex residing in him- or herself, as well as the spontaneously expressed traits of one's own sex.

The Chinese too, since ancient times, recognized this necessity. It is their concept—that wholeness consists of the balanced interplay of the yin and yang forces—that is the motif of the Korean flag that was dramatically placed before me in this coincidence. *Yin* is feminine, yielding, receptive, negative, dark, the unconscious:

symbolic of the fruitful earth. *Yang* is masculine, strong, active, penetrating, consciousness, light: symbolic of heaven. The Taoist philosophical perspective sees all of creation as the admixture of yin and yang, negative and positive, feminine and masculine, in varying degrees.

As my life proceeded, I continued to investigate Eastern philosophy and metaphysics, especially Taoism, with its perpetual interplay of yin and yang. A dozen years later, this led me to study tai chi with a Chinese master in New York, for tai chi is considered a practical application of knowledge of the harmonious interaction of yin and yang. Then, a couple of years after that, I enrolled in graduate school to study East Asian philosophy and metaphysics.

In other ways too, my exploration of the intuitive Eastern tendencies has flourished in concert with the rational tendencies of the masculine West. For instance, a few years after returning home, I wrote a small book on dream analysis at the request of a friend in publishing, as my interest in the symbolic expressions of the unconscious continued to bloom.

Yet the symbolic expression of meaning was increasingly seen to extend beyond the subconscious realm of dreams, to situations in the waking state. This recognition led to my appreciation of the roles of mirror coincidences and directional coincidences in our lives.

I have encountered numerous directional coincidences since that first one recalled in Korea. Many have repeated the same theme so eloquently expressed there. The rest of this section (on directional coincidences experienced along the path of life) will focus on a few that reinforced the theme of the one above.

Before going on to other coincidences, I would like to point out that secondary details in a coincidence (just as in a dream) can provide significant, although more subtle meaning. Certainly, in the preceding coincidence, it is easy to see the significance of the two flags, the two anthems, the two of us, the yin and yang symbols, and the one round red sun. But there is another factor that provides direction in that coincidence, which was unrecognized until recently.

In recalling this coincidence, it occurred to me that I was not wearing a uniform. Although I was the military man—the supposed warrior—I was in civilian clothes, while my friend wore the uniform of a monk: plain white robes. Warriorship is not intrinsically about combating an enemy; it is about discipline, integrity, commitment, and marshaling all of one's resources toward the attainment or defense of an ideal. This is the goal of the warrior monk, the spiritual warrior.

The fact that the monk was in uniform, and I was not, likely conveyed meaning. I realized that, although I was a military officer, I was not all that disciplined, or even totally committed to any cause. I had long been aware that I needed more discipline and a more thorough sense of commitment if I were to achieve the things important to me. If I were to realize that sound, symmetrical, vibrant, wholeness symbolized by the round, red sun, my discipline and commitment had to be much more thorough. The uniformed monk, the spiritual warrior, was much more the warrior than I.

As the role of the Buddhist monk in this coincidence illustrates, other people are components of coincidences and dreams for a reason. There are generally two ways another person in a coincidence may be symbolic.

An individual may personify for you a particular quality or characteristic, such as compassion, aggressiveness, self-discipline, deceit, loyalty, and so on. It is the quality the individual represents that is pertinent in the coincidence, reflecting one of your qualities that needs to be addressed. A positive quality may need to be nurtured, or a negative quality diminished. The uniformed monk symbolized for me warriorship—particularly spiritual warriorship—a quality that I needed to cultivate.

If the most prominent thing that comes to mind when you think of your Aunt Abigail is her unconditional love, she may very well symbolize that quality for you. If she is a component of a coincidence (or dream), it is likely she is there to convey a message about such pure love. On the other hand, if Uncle Al is notoriously self-centered, his role in a coincidence may well convey a message about being egotistical. The specific relevance of the quality in question should be revealed by the details of the coincidence or dream.

A person may also be significant by simply representing a particular previous situation that he or she was a part of. For example, if it was at Zelda's New Year's Eve party that your husband proposed to you, she may represent for you that important event.

A final consideration about another's role in our coincidence is whether his or her words spoken in association with the coincidence have more significance than we would normally attribute to them. The coincidence may serve to highlight the importance of what has been said.

Buried Treasure Unearthed

A small, dark, antique bottle provided me with a coincidence many years ago that I still look back upon to reestablish my sense of direction. I found it a few years after returning to the United States, when a large part of my energies continued to be focused upon exploring and nurturing the Eastern mind-set; the focus of my reading was Eastern philosophy and metaphysics. I continued to flirt with meditation. I consciously cultivated an awareness of oneness with the beauty and mystery of nature. And the analysis of dreams for exploration of the unconscious continued to be a fertile pursuit.

My home, at the time, was in the Berkshire Mountains of western Connecticut. I was preparing my vegetable garden for planting when I unearthed the bottle from the dark loam. What grasped my attention about this small bottle, which looked like it might have once contained medicine or a "miracle" remedy, were the letters embossed upon it: *BELL—ANS*. I immediately perceived *ANS* as an abbreviation for answer. This very unusual inscription, containing my name, seemed to convey "the answer for Bell"—my answer.

What was Bell's answer? The original medicinal contents of this small, dark amber bottle had long since been expended. It now contained rich earth—the same dark, fertile loam that had concealed it in my garden.

The dark earth symbolizes the unconscious—deep, mysterious, and unfathomable—in contrast to consciousness, which is above the surface and visible. It symbolizes nature's feminine creative aspect, for it is the womb of life, just as the unconscious is the fertile ground from which the structures and ideas of the conscious mind emerge. The earth is also the breast that nurtures all living things. Both the birthing and nurturing qualities of the earth are underscored by the activity I was engaged in: planting seeds from which nourishing food grows, just as the seeds for my growth and fruition lay in the rich nurturing depths of the unconscious mind.

The depth and wealth of the unconscious is revealed, for example, in Carl Jung's concept of the collective unconscious, which we each possess deep within us, containing in symbolic form all of humankind's deep-seated knowledge inherited from antiquity. Jung's concept may have been inspired by the concept of supreme consciousness of Hindu metaphysics: God's absolute, infinite consciousness (*chit*), which may be tapped by going deep within the unconscious mind in meditation.

Bell's answer—my answer—was found by tilling the earth, which brought it to the surface. This directional coincidence said to me that my answer, my medicine—the key to my happiness, health, and fruition—was to be found in tilling the unconscious (the dark earth in the bottle, which the bottle was also in). Again, this is the mindset of the East. It is the yin side of the dynamic, balanced circle of yin and yang forces. For yin is dark, receptive, intuitive, fertile, nurturing, and symbolized by the earth.

Fulfillment would be attained by bringing to the surface (to the light of consciousness) that which was contained within. This reinforced the meditation, dream analysis, and exploration of the depth of humankind, and it encouraged nurturance of the tender romanticist. Over the years, that dark amber bottle unearthed in my garden, which I have before me now, has continued to inspire me to follow this path.

More Treasure Unearthed

Later, I encountered another coincidence in the garden that supports the first one and also the importance of the warrior posture suggested in the initial coincidence in this section. Additionally, it bears mention because it is similar to a type of coincidence that just about everyone has experienced. That is the type in which a thought suddenly enters one's mind for no apparent reason and then is immediately followed by an experience that reflects the thought.

The most common example of this is when we think of someone (perhaps a relative or friend who hasn't been heard from in months or years). Just then, the phone rings, and it is that person on the line. It is one of those coincidences in which you seem to be exhibiting powers of extrasensory perception. But if ESP is not a regular part of your repertoire, it must be viewed as either a mirror or directional coincidence.

We are aware that, if an area of the psyche is charged, a mirror coincidence may occur that reflects the area of concern. If you had been thinking about the person, with deep feeling, perhaps repeatedly, then a call, a letter, or an unexpected encounter with that person may constitute a mirror coincidence. If there is a particular situation or concern gripping you, the individual may be associated with some aspect of that concern.

We know from past examples that a mirror coincidence may spill over into the directional realm. Therefore, even if the coincidence is the reflection of a charged complex, it may also serve as a directional coincidence. On the other hand, if an open appraisal of your psychological state doesn't reveal a related area of heightened concern, the coincidence is likely purely directional.

The following coincidence is similar to those in which a thought spontaneously comes to mind, immediately followed by an encounter with the subject of the thought. The difference in my case is that it does not involve a person, but an object.

The second coincidence involving unearthed treasure happened when I was walking toward the far end of my garden. Totally spontaneously, I stated to the person beside me, "You know, one of these days I'm going to find an arrowhead in this garden." Once the words left my mouth, I looked down to notice a white quartz arrowhead nearly fully revealed in the earth, and concluded with "And here it is!" At the time, I was both very pleased with the find and mystified about how it had taken place.

A great many arrowheads, as well as other Indian artifacts, have been found in the plowed fields of southern New England. Many people have built up respectable collections of artifacts simply by walking through fields after they have been plowed in the spring. Furthermore, when Europeans first settled the land, a Native American village was situated on the banks of the river that flows by the property I owned. So the surprising thing was not that the arrowhead was found, but that it was found just when it occurred to me that one would be found.

Some of the groundwork for its meaning was laid in the previous coincidence, when we looked at what the earth symbolizes. The key to additional meaning is the significance of the arrow, of which the quartz head is the only part that would not have decomposed over time. This is one of those instances where the meaning of a *universal symbol* applies, in addition to the meaning more particularly related to the individual (in this case me), causing it to also function as a *personal symbol*.

From far antiquity to recent times, arrows have played a vital role for humankind. It is not surprising that they have deep-seated meaning, as expressed in myths, literature, and art. Arrows are weapons, used in hunting, personal protection, and warfare. As such, the arrow represents the warrior and his power, which is reinforced by the phallic symbolism inherent in its shape.

In motion, an arrow is swift and straight. In mythology, the arrow is the weapon of Apollo, the sun god. In the depths of our unconscious, it symbolizes the rays of the sun in being swift, straight, powerful, and penetrating. In this capacity, it symbolizes the supreme power of God's illuminating consciousness, which in humanity is the mind's penetrating power of illumination.

It is easy to see how the symbolic meaning of the discovery of the arrowhead, which had been unearthed from the dark soil, is similar to that of the previous coincidence. They both address the potency of tilling the unconscious, to bring the penetrating knowledge hidden there to light.

For me, though, personal associations with the warrior imagery raised by the arrowhead heightened its meaning. My great-grandmother was a Native American of the Massachuset Federation, a

descendant of some of the few not massacred in the appropria-
tion of the land by "civilized" people. I believe it is primarily
because of my love and respect for nature, and my desire to com-
mune with her in intimate harmony, that I have long identified
with the "Indian" warrior in me. The Native American warrior
adhered to a principled relationship with nature, which embodied
deep respect and appreciation.

The depth of the warrior aspect of myself was revealed to me
later in a dream. On this occasion, as I was about to go to sleep, I
asked my unconscious to provide me with a dream that would
explain something that was happening in my life. Specifically, I
was overwhelmed by the fact that my first marriage was ending in
divorce and wished to know why it was happening to me. What
was the meaning of it all?

In response, I did have a dream, although it more clearly illustrated *what* was happening, rather than *why* it was happening. In
this dream, I was an imposing warrior with a bow and quiver of
arrows, striding through the fields and forests I used to roam when
I was growing up. At one point, my two young sons were with me.
Then they were not. At one point, my ex-wife was also there. After
she was gone, I noticed my arrows were missing from the quiver
that had contained them, and I realized she had stolen them. The
dream then ended with a strong sense of vulnerability for my sons
and me in the face of an unseen hostile entity, which I could not
combat.

The metaphor of the stolen arrows presents a good example of
a principle we will discuss later, the conservation of symbols, in
which one symbol in a particular situation possesses two or more
distinct and relevant meanings. In its most universal and clearest
meaning, the stolen arrows represent an emasculation of the warrior's power and vitality. Without arrows, the warrior's effectiveness is severely handicapped. The emasculation was conveyed quite
graphically, in that the stolen arrows are phallic in shape and also
in their function of penetration.

In the previously noted association with the sun's rays, arrows
are symbolic of the sun's powers of illumination and procreation,
the latter in the sense that it is the light and warmth of the rays of

the sun penetrating the earth that results in its fertility. This phallic imagery again reinforces the symbolic association between arrows and the sun's rays. In this context, the theft of the arrows may be considered a theft of an individual's powers of illumination, the penetrating power of discovery and revelation of knowledge.

The meanings of the theft of the arrows as a universal symbol did apply. While dealing with the trauma of the disintegration of my immediate family, my warrior-like quest for enlightenment and illumination of the underlying meaning and purpose of life, along with my physical and psychological vitality, was temporarily lost.

Through the conservation of symbols, the theft of the arrows also possessed meaning for me as a personal symbol. On this level, it represented my two young sons being taken from me. After all, an arrow (♂) is the symbol for the male. The context of the dream, in association with the circumstances that stimulated it, reveals that the arrows being taken from me were a personal symbol for my sons, who were likewise effectively taken from my home.

To return to the directional coincidence of the arrowhead discovered in my garden, it is the meaning of arrows as universal symbols, particularly the warrior aspect of the symbolism, that is relevant. The type of warriorship I am referring to is the type addressed in the coincidence with the Buddhist monk. It is also that which Chogyam Trungpa advocates in his book, *Shambhala: The Sacred Path of the Warrior*. Coincidentally, Chogyam Trungpa was also a Buddhist monk; therefore, we can be sure that what he advocates—the sacred path of the warrior—is not about warfare or aggression.

In the foreword, he states that "this book is a manual for people who have lost the principles of sacredness, dignity, and warriorship in their lives. . . . This book shows how to refine one's way of life and how to propagate the true meaning of warriorship" (Trungpa 1984, xix). Trungpa says there is a basic human wisdom that can help solve our problems, which is particularly embodied in the principles of warriorship of ancient India, Tibet, China, Japan, and Korea. Yet, "This wisdom does not belong to any one culture or religion, nor does it come only from the West or the East. Rather, it is a tradition of human warriorship that has existed in many cultures at many times throughout history" (Trungpa 1984, 5).

A true warrior maintains an unswerving adherence to the principles he or she regards as worthy, regardless of personal consequences. The warrior possesses an ingrained, unalterable commitment to "do the right thing" in regard to his or her fellow human beings, and all of creation, including her- or himself. The warrior is an idealist, fearless in the quest to make real what is the ideal. All personal considerations are secondary to discovering and actualizing the particular ideals that are personally suitable for the warrior to embody. The warrior is on a quest of discovery, seeking the foundations of truth and love, which, when found, will never be relinquished, regardless of personal consequences. So, the warrior first seeks the ethical principles that provide enduring happiness and fulfillment and then is adamant in adhering to them. In all these facets, the warrior is a person of self-discipline.

The meaning of the directional coincidence of discovering the arrowhead unearthed in my garden, just when I had articulated my sudden sense that I would find one, should now be more apparent. Like the previous coincidence, it directed me to look within to the fertile ground of the unconscious mind in the quest for illumination and fruition, but also to look within for the source of discipline and the power to persevere on that quest in spite of the obstacles encountered along the way.

When Plums Were Prunes

The last coincidence in this section is included because it vigorously supports a posture that must be maintained if we are to fully benefit from directional coincidences. It reinforces the effectiveness of possessing the true humility required to subdue the arrogance of the ego, so that we may respond to the guidance presented in our everyday world.

In the mid-1980s, I attended graduate school for a couple of years, while simultaneously working full-time. A course in oriental religion required an oral presentation and a paper on a topic of the student's choice. I decided to do a presentation on the *Tao Te Ching*, the concise Chinese classic that is the cornerstone of the

philosophical perspective known as Taoism and the most translated of all Chinese works.

The Tao is usually translated as "the Way," referring to the way
creation unfolds and operates. It is similar to, but not the same as,
the Western conception of God. The most obvious difference is
that the Tao is not a being, or very being-like. It may be viewed as
an unfathomable, omnipresent force. A good definition of the Tao
is the following: the indivisible One, which is both the one primordial energy and one primordial principle, underlying, and
comprising in its myriad variations, all of creation.

Te is the specific expression of Tao inherent and natural to a
particular thing—that which provides it with its virtue, character,
and strength. In a human being, *te* is achieved by ensuring that the
subtle power of the Tao within oneself remains unconstricted by
the plans and schemes of the ego. The *Tao Te Ching* describes the
Tao (the reality behind and within creation) and its ideal operation
(te) in the individual.

Many scholars recognize that the *Tao Te Ching*, which reputedly
was written by the sage Lao Tzu around 400 BCE, possesses addi-
tions and amplifications that would not have been in the original
work. I perceived differences in style, rhythm, and philosophical
perspective, and explanations that must have been amplifications
by later scholars. So I decided to do what scholars for over two
thousand years had not seen fit to do. I would strip this work of all
counterfeit material, to present the "real" *Tao Te Ching*.

The coincidence was precipitated by my decision to enhance
my presentation by bringing an antique statue of the mythical
Chinese god of longevity to class. His long ears and high-domed,
bald head symbolize longevity and wisdom. His right hand holds
a staff to which a scroll is tied, to symbolize virtuous, lawful conduct. And a peach, symbolizing the heart, is held against his chest
to represent his intimate grasp of the heart of compassion and
wisdom. The heart plays a very important role in the mystical traditions of China, India, and the rest of Asia. In addition to its common association with love and compassion, mystics view it as the
abode of transcendental wisdom and supreme consciousness.

The statue's look of inscrutable wisdom reminded me of the

author of the *Tao Te Ching*, Lao Tzu, as did its long ears. For Lao Tzu, which is an affectionate name for an elder, means "long ears."

However, I had trouble with the idea of the heart's being symbolized by a peach. I didn't recall seeing peach trees in Japan or Korea, although plum trees were common. In addition, I had noticed some marvelous, large, dark-red plums in the Korean vegetable markets that now abound in Manhattan. In color and texture of skin, they seemed to me to more closely resemble the heart. So I decided it was more likely that a plum was held in the hand of the sage. My intention was to purchase enough plums to pass out to my dozen classmates, to illustrate graphically the similarity in shape, color, and texture between a plum and a heart.

When the day of my presentation arrived, I allowed sufficient time before class to purchase the wonderful plums.

However, the first Korean market I went to had only a few plums, and they were alarmingly small and scrawny. The next market had an ample supply, but again they were all of this small variety, which appeared nearly all skin and pit. For the first time in all the times I had visited these markets, the wonderfully large plums were nowhere to be seen.

After checking another market, I realized they would not be found. If I had been more open and flexible, I could have abandoned the use of plums. Instead, I purchased the scrawny plums, and with a sense of impending doom proceeded to class. Aware of the meaningful nature of coincidences, I was concerned that this unexpected problem might foreshadow difficulties with my presentation. The inadequacy of the plums might reflect a meager insufficiency, instead of a fullness and richness, of my report.

My worst fears were realized. The embarrassment over the size and condition of the plums as a symbol of the heart was minor compared to the professor's response once it became clear that I intended to present the "real" *Tao Te Ching*. Since I had only begun to study the Chinese language, and had not yet studied ancient Chinese at all, I had obviously not read the work in the original language. Thus, I was unqualified to make such a paring. I was not even allowed to proceed with the presentation.

In this coincidence, my arrogance and lack of humility were

twice highlighted. The difficulty it got me into when I substituted the peach that traditionally symbolizes the heart, for the plum which appealed more to me, foreshadowed the difficulty caused by my attempt to do what scholars (who actually had the technical background to attempt it) had for thousands of years not seen fit to do. To make amends for my arrogance, I decided the subject of my paper should be the Humility of the *Tao*, as expressed in the *Tao Te Ching*.

My decision was not made simply because my actions pointed to the need to cultivate humility. The humility of the *Tao*, and of the sage who personifies it, is a prevalent theme of the *Tao Te Ching*. Humility's role is introduced with six eloquent stances. Speaking of the *Tao*, the second verse says:

> The myriad creatures rise from it yet it claims no authority;
> It gives them life yet claims no possession;
> It benefits them yet exacts no gratitude;
> It accomplishes its task yet lays claim to no merit;
> It is because it lays claim to no merit
> that its merit never deserts it. (Lau 1997, 5)

The Tao claims no authority, no possession, no gratitude, no merit. It creates the musicians and the instruments, and composes and orchestrates the sublime symphony, yet claims no benefit or recognition. In a word, it is humble. The sage, whose embrace of the Tao provides his power and virtue (*Te*), must then reflect these same qualities. Verse 39 says:

> The Master views the parts with compassion,
> because he understands the whole.
> His constant practice is humility.
> He doesn't glitter like a jewel
> but lets himself be shaped by the Tao. (Mitchell 1988, 39)

Ultimately, exercising the humility to learn from this directional coincidence did enable me to receive a very good grade on my paper. Yet the real importance of the coincidence is that it underscores the unequaled practical value of having the humility to allow oneself to "be shaped by the Tao," which is the essential truth this book attempts to convey: the person who puts his or her ego and limited intelligence aside, to be guided by the directional coincidences that are a product of the sublime intelligence of God, will attain success.

Finally, a lesson about symbol analysis is also contained in this coincidence. In analyzing a symbol, all essential qualities should be considered. By designating the plum as the symbol of the heart, I ignored the fact that, in size, peaches clearly more closely resemble the heart.

DIRECTIONAL COINCIDENCE AND THIS BOOK

Directional coincidences do not happen once in a decade, or every few years, or maybe one a year. A very important point that must be established about directional coincidences is that they will consistently occur when needed, if we are receptive to their guidance. There were many uncertainties for me associated with writing this book, including the specific content, its manner of presentation, and whether to make the project my full-time vocation. I have encountered (and continue to encounter) many coincidences providing valuable help toward the success of this project.

Most directional coincidences are not sensational. They are usually subtle. If we are not aware of the way guidance may be provided through events in our natural world, many coincidences might easily go unrecognized. To illustrate that subtle directional coincidences do take place on regular basis, here are a few of the many I have encountered that relate specifically to writing this book.

A Great Idea

One coincidence occurred as I was walking through Kennedy Park, pulling my sea kayak behind me en route to watch the sunrise on adjacent Biscayne Bay. I have a set of wheels like those on a golf cart, which may be placed under one end of the kayak and secured with bungee cords, allowing me to pull the kayak with the handle on the bow. I usually ride my bike, with kayak in tow, the few blocks to the ocean. But my bike had a flat tire, so I was walking that day.

There was an issue troubling me that I intended to contemplate on the water as the sun emerged from the ocean. I hoped the expansiveness and clarity of the ocean sunrise would likewise promote clarity in my thoughts.

In fact, before I even got to the bay, while briskly striding in hope of entering the water before the sun first peeked above the surface, I reached a tentative solution to the issue that concerned me. I had intended to present the theories and experimental results of modern physics as the primary source for the metaphysical basis of coincidences. This was in spite of the fact that I viewed the similar perspectives on the foundations of reality held by mystics, particularly those of the East, to be more authoritative, consistent, comprehensive, and correct.

I felt that even spiritually inclined readers might give the theories of Western science far more credibility than the time-worn and time-tested realizations of the mystic. However, I was not sure that was the best approach and was uncomfortable with my intention. On the way to the bay, I decided not to slight the mystics's comprehension of reality, but give the reader the opportunity to consider the merits of their recognitions. Western science would be assigned a supporting and substantiating role.

With kayak in tow, I navigated the macadam path through the ocean front park, while enthusiastically reflecting on the correctness of this approach—thinking to myself, "That's a great idea!" Just then I encountered a couple passing in the opposite direction. As I looked up, the man, with clear intelligent eyes looked directly into mine, and eagerly declared, "That's a great idea."

He, of course, was not referring to my idea. Assuming he lacked ESP, he was obviously referring either to my means of transporting the kayak or to the idea of the imminent voyage. Yet the coincidence that he vocalized the very thoughts that were simultaneously in my mind, I took to be *directional.* The fact that moments later I was successful in getting afloat just in time to see the sun emerge, certainly did not diminish my appreciation that the man's endorsement was a coincidence providing guidance that my new approach was correct.

A similar coincidence, in which an impromptu remark of another reinforced prospective content, occurred at the end of a phone conversation with Wendy. She was staying at my mother's house for a day or so because her work required her to be in that area. While meditating earlier that morning, an idea for a concept to include in the book spontaneously emerged from some recess of my mind. It was to use the bell curve—which is a graph of the standard distribution of some variable in a population—to illustrate how directional coincidences can help us move toward the smaller percentages of the culture who are very content with the quality of their lives.

In a conversation with Wendy some months earlier, I had used the bell curve in a similar analogy in regard to the evolution of the quality of our relationship. Then, on the morning of our phone conversation, as we were saying goodbye she suddenly said, "Oh, have you seen the book *The Bell Curve*?" She had noticed the book the night before while browsing in a local bookstore. I responded with, "What a coincidence," and told her of the idea that had occurred to me earlier in the morning while meditating. Partially due to this coincidence, the bell curve plays an important role in chapter four, *Coincidence and the Quality of Life.*

This type of directional coincidence is fairly common. The words of strangers, or an associate or relative, in unconnected conversation often provide the solution to a problem that had been gripping another.

Throw Away the Books on This One

I am grateful for one coincidence which gave assurance that putting all my apples in one basket, the book-writing basket, was correct. One of the difficult decisions regarding this project was simply to embark on it as my sole vocation, and then have the courage to continue. It required me, at least temporarily, to abandon a fairly well-paying career, with the knowledge that the longer

I remained away the less marketable my skills would be. It required using financial resources intended for retirement, at a time of life when people invest most heavily for retirement. Finally, there was and is no guarantee the book will be purchased by a publisher.

This book was originally begun a couple of years ago as a part-time endeavor, while still pursuing my longtime career as an airline pilot. After my half-dozen years in the Air Force, I joined the pilot ranks of one of the world's largest international airlines, which nearly two decades later went out of business. I then flew for one of the world's smallest international airlines, which necessitated a commute from my home in Miami to New York. Unfortunately, with the time and energy that work and the commute demanded, this project had to be set aside.

Since I viewed this as such a worthy endeavor, my inability to pursue it nagged me. I often asserted to Wendy that I was going to resume writing, but could never find the time. Then a major expansion at work was canceled, which provided an opportunity for me to resign with some nice financial incentives to do so. So, with Wendy's enthusiastic encouragement, I decided to take a year or so off from flying, to attempt to bring the importance of coincidence to light. I hoped to embark on a new career that was more in harmony with the interests I had been drawn to for so many years.

In the early stages, I was very often consumed with doubt about the course I had taken. Sometimes what I had written would prove disappointing. Frequently, a major expense, such as for my son's college, would cause anxiety about diminishing material resources. At other times, a friend might inform me of an airline that was looking for pilots with my qualifications, or I might receive notice from an airline of their pilot needs. I questioned whether I was being responsible and realistic in devoting all my resources to this project, rather than hedging my bets by again attempting to both fly and write.

One day, with these thoughts not foremost in my mind but lurking in some recess, I took a needed break from my cloistered activity to go for a walk around the neighborhood. That particular day, as I strolled along a narrow lane admiring the lush vegetation that abounds in my neighborhood, I was very surprised to encounter a couple of stacks of large books.

The books, all in excellent condition, were lying in the grass beside the road. The larger stack contained perhaps seven books, with a few more in the smaller one. The only title I noticed was the one on the topmost book of the large stack. In large prominent letters it read *Financial Accounting*. The large books all appeared to be textbooks in excellent condition, and thus—as anyone who has had to buy them knows—worth a lot of money.

When a very unusual circumstance like this is unexpectedly encountered, I approach it as a possible coincidence. The fact that the situation probably has a logical explanation (for instance, that the books were overlooked in the process of moving) doesn't negate the fact that to one encountering the scene, it is very unusual and a bit bizarre.

The circumstance that the most prominently displayed textbook, and the only one revealing a title, was emblazoned with *Financial Accounting*, a topic of considerable concern for me, led me to conclude that here was a directional coincidence dealing with that subject. The problem was to determine its meaning, about which I was uncertain.

In my state of general anxiety over financial matters, my initial interpretation of meaning was pessimistic. With the books standing out so prominently in that setting and the words *financial accounting* so conspicuous, I feared the direction presented was to pay attention to financial accounting, to "tend to the books" on the subject.

This illustrates the need for an important caution when analyzing symbolic situations in dreams or coincidences. We must be careful not to impose meaning that reflects either fears and anxieties, or hopes and expectations instead of that which the symbolic situation objectively conveys.

When I was able to look at the situation objectively, I realized that the meaning is rather straightforward. It is true the books stood out, especially the one titled *Financial Accounting*, but there was nothing to suggest this meant they should be studied more diligently.

The most unusual and prominent circumstance was the appearance that the textbooks had been abandoned. In seeking symbolic significance we can look to expressions such as "throw away the books" or "we can't go by the books on this one," in reference to the means of achieving a desired goal or solving a problem.

The symbolic meaning of a roadway is also important. The discarded books were not, for instance, in a field, or a trash can, or in front of a library, but by the roadside. The most common symbolic use of a road or path is to convey our journey through life. Take, for instance, Frank Sinatra's question of "who knows where the road may lead us" or Robert Frost's moving poem about taking the path less traveled.

The logical meaning of encountering the abandoned textbooks by the roadside was that I was being directed to "throw away the book" on financial matters. At least in this portion of my journey, I could discard *conventional wisdom* on the correct and responsible way to approach financial concerns.

Furthermore, this disregard of conventional wisdom may extend into other unspecified areas, since there were other unidentified textbooks discarded by the roadway. In fact, *Comprehending Coincidence* certainly departs from the traditional perspective of reality, which may in part be represented by the subject matter of the other abandoned textbooks.

I am pleased to report that, since a day or two after this coincidence, when I went beyond my fears to analyze the symbolism correctly, I have shed much of the anxiety previously experienced about financial concerns. As of now though, the jury is still out. The correctness of my interpretation of this directional coincidence remains to be confirmed. However, if you are reading this in a book about coincidence, there is some evidence the interpretation is correct.

Hi-Tech Coincidence

With the hours upon hours I have spent punching these words out on the keyboard of a computer, it is not surprising that my laptop has been the vehicle for directional coincidences. The meaning of one that surfaced as a persistent and mysterious glitch was relatively easy to establish.

There is a very wise and loving woman who serves as my spiritual mentor and guide, as she does for thousands of other people of various religious persuasions around the world. Her name is Gurumayi Chidvilasananda. The second half of chapter four of this book consists of a section entitled "Humans Who Have Achieved Human Potential." Gurumayi is one such as those presented there, for she has fully developed the depth of human resources that we each have the potential to actualize. Prior to embarking on this project full-time, I was fortunate to have an opportunity to ask Gurumayi if I should do so. I told her that I had begun the book earlier but, with the demands of work, had not been able to continue. I came away feeling I had Gurumayi's strong encouragement to write the book, and that her implication was that my personal resources were more needed in this capacity, than for flying a plane. Without Gurumayi's encouragement, I would not have had the courage to give up flying in order to complete this endeavor.

In gratitude for all her compassionate tutelage, I declared my indebtedness to Gurumayi in the last paragraph of the first page of an early version of the introduction. For some mysterious reason, I had great difficulty keeping that paragraph on the first page. Whenever I turned the computer on or returned to the first page from later material, I would find that the paragraph had jumped to the second page, leaving a conspicuously large gap at the bottom of the first page. I would then reposition the paragraph to the first page, and "save" it in that position, only to later find that it had again jumped to the second page.

I tried reducing the words, widening the margins, and decreasing the bottom margin, all of which worked temporarily. But no matter what I attempted, when I later returned to the first page, the entire last paragraph (not just a sentence or two) had jumped to the second page.

I eventually speculated that the mysterious behavior of my computer might comprise a directional coincidence. The first page of the introduction is probably the most conspicuous page in a book. It is the first place most people look to appraise or get to know a book. The mention there of gratitude to a swami from India could make a Western reader or prospective publisher uncomfortable, and foster misconceptions about the nature of this work.

The strange behavior of my computer, in stimulating those concerns, induced me to eliminate the disappearing paragraph. Once that was accomplished, I had no more difficulty keeping the subsequent paragraph on the first page.

Since you, the reader, have by now become familiar with this investigation, I can comfortably mention this directional coincidence here. By now, if I have been successful, you should be aware that this is a substantive work, which will stand up well to critical appraisal. Therefore, my indebtedness to a great being from the East should not cause alarm, even to those people who distrust cultural traditions not indigenous to the West. My intention here is not to express my deep gratitude toward Gurumayi, but to illustrate that, in addition to directional coincidences that encouraged specific content of this book, others have discouraged inclusion of material where it was inappropriate.

What You Want Versus What You Need

In their popular song of a couple of decades ago, Mick Jagger and The Rolling Stones insightfully insisted that, while you can't always get what you want, you somehow manage to get what you need. I was fortunate to have that truth reinforced in the following directional coincidence.

Two components considered desirable, if not necessary, for the successful publication of a book are the knowledgeable critique of the work by someone with editorial skills and representation by a good literary agent. At the time of this coincidence, I had access to neither.

The spatial coordinates of the coincidence extend from Miami to Los Angeles, and to the skies between Los Angeles and New York. It is a coincidence in which Wendy is a key participant. It began with a phone call from Wendy in Los Angeles to me in Miami. Perhaps you have figured out Wendy's occupation. She is a flight attendant for one of the country's largest airlines.

Wendy called from Los Angeles before leaving the hotel for an all-night flight back to New York. In our conversation, I happened to mention my perception that a key component to getting this book published might be finding a literary agent to represent me. It is true that, at that point in the evolution of the work, I was much more in need of competent editorial help; but I was not aware of the extent of that need. I was more concerned about finding a literary agent.

My problem, as I perceived it, was that I was quite in the dark about how to go about finding an agent. Yet, just a few hours after our conversation, by coincidence, Wendy was directed to an agent who provided the assistance I most urgently needed, although not what I wanted.

One of the few virtues of an all night flight, from the perspective of both passengers and flight attendants, is that most of the passengers are able to sleep for much of the flight. This leaves the flight attendants free to read, chat, or eat at their leisure.

Of course, there are always a few passengers who are too caught up in concerns or too excited about life to sleep. When Wendy, who was working the first-class section, roamed to the back to visit with other crew members, she found one of the stay-awake passengers helping the flight attendants pass the time. Proficient with tarot cards, he was entertaining some of them by giving readings. Not being a fan of the tarot, Wendy declined his offer for a reading and returned to the front of the plane. Yet it was not long before she returned to consult him on a different matter.

One of the flight attendants meandered up to first-class and mentioned that the guy doing the tarot readings was an author. Wendy, who is pretty sharp even at two or three in the morning, immediately thought the author might have an agent he could recommend. She returned to the aft cabin and found out he was returning home from a promotional tour for a recently published science fiction novel. She asked if he had an agent. He replied that he not only had an agent, he was married to her. Wendy informed him that I was writing a book on coincidence and was hoping to find an agent. He gave her his wife's card and said I should call her.

When Wendy related these events, I enthusiastically thought that perhaps my concerns about finding a literary agent were solved.

The coincidence of Wendy's unexpectedly being referred to a literary agent on the evening I told her that it was important to secure the services of one might provide the solution to my problem. When Wendy returned home and gave me the agent's card, I carefully filed it in a safe place. My intention had long been to wait until I had finished the first three chapters before contacting an agent. I was very pleased to have a lead to pursue once that was accomplished.

A couple of months later, having completed the initial version of the first few chapters, I summoned the courage to call the literary agent in New York. I was encouraged to hear that she recalled her husband's mention of meeting Wendy, and that she would take a look at the chapters completed thus far. With high hopes, I printed my unfinished manuscript, and sent it up the coast to New York.

The agent's response revealed that some serious editing and rewriting was certainly the most critical need. Surely the search for an agent and/or publisher should not be pursued until the manuscript was in a more finished form.

Her critique of the work and suggested improvements provided very needed information to this neophyte writer about what was required to make it more polished and palatable. Among her suggestions were to break down the chapters with headings, make the work more autobiographical, and make it clearer, simpler, and more reader-friendly.

She said she could refer me to *professional writers* who could help polish the work, which prompted me to go over it with a more discriminating eye. In doing so, I became increasingly appalled at how dense and rough it was. I had been so consumed with the daunting task of just getting ideas and experiences of this extraordinary phenomenon on paper that I had sorely neglected to critically appraise the quality of my writing.

I am grateful that, just hours after I mentioned the need for a literary agent, Wendy happened to encounter the agent's husband. It turned out that the knowledgeable suggestions and critique provided by the agent were urgently needed. I was in the dark about where I could find someone with appropriate editorial skills and the extent of the need for those skills. I was provided with a directional coincidence that offered guidance for what I most needed, not what I thought I needed most.

No News is Good News

After I became thoroughly engaged in writing this book, it became apparent that time had to be managed well if I were to be successful in such a formidable task. I do not write fast, and at least a couple of revisions are usually necessary to make the material fairly readable. Research can also be very time-consuming. In my case, however, the importance of deferring leisure activities in favor of effective time management provided added impetus from a directional coincidence.

One activity critically appraised in terms of time taken from writing and research was the procurement of "news." Fortunately, I have long considered local television news to be engaged primarily in pandering and cheap sensationalism. And even network news seems to me to have become repetitive and frequently sensationalist driven. However, a newspaper is a different story.

Although the majority is no less guilty of sensationalism and superficiality, at least with a newspaper you can read what you want when you want to, instead of being at the mercy of another's decision of when you may view what they choose for your viewing pleasure. One may also ignore advertisements, as well as the most offensive stories. In spite of those virtues, it was not too difficult to kick a mild addiction to the daily paper, in acceptance of the need to employ time more wisely.

However, the Sunday paper was a little more challenging. The luxury of a leisurely breakfast, perhaps even in bed, with the paper spread all about to be casually explored, was not easily relinquished. For a while, this sacred pastime still retained a treasured niche in my weekly activities, even though I increasingly viewed it from the production manager's perspective of being largely a waste of time.

The directional coincidence began one Sunday some months ago when I snatched four quarters, jumped into the car, and headed to the nearest paper machine, which was empty. A block or two away there was another machine, which I was relieved to note had papers left. Although the paper seemed lighter than normal, I did not notice until I got home that it was Saturday's paper, which, uncharacteristically, I happened to have read.

After relating the situation to Wendy, I grabbed my wallet and headed for the nearby "E Z Kwik Kuntry Store." While en route, it occurred to me that what happened might be a directional coincidence and that I probably should not be getting a paper. But I was determined to complete my mission anyway. When I got to the store, there were stacks of papers, and they were even Sunday papers. I checked. However when I went to pay for the paper I was dismayed, and amused, to find I had no cash in my wallet. I belatedly recalled that the previous evening I had taken the money out of it so I would not have to carry the wallet when we went out for pizza.

By now I was about ninety-five percent sure that the obstacles to buying a Sunday paper comprised a directional coincidence that encouraged a more fruitful use of time. Still, I pondered whether I would get some cash when I got home, in order to stubbornly continue the paper-purchasing mission. However, the store owner relieved me of that decision by suggesting I take the paper and pay him another time.

I realize that someone who has not examined coincidences for decades, and had meaning repeatedly reinforced, might not attribute as much significance to those series of events as I do. For me, the guidance was adequate and the discouraged activity sufficiently uncontroversial to prohibit the waste of time reading a Sunday paper for a couple of months.

Then, one Sunday, we decided to splurge and have brunch at one of the sidewalk cafes on Ocean Drive in South Beach. Afterward, in keeping with the tone that had been set, I thought, "Oh, well, what's the harm of getting a Sunday paper once in a while." So, we stopped at a convenience store, where I purchased a paper to read when we got home.

Less than two-and-a-half hours later, I received a call from my credit card company, informing me that they had noticed some unusual activity on my card, and, as a security precaution, wanted to ensure the card had not been lost or stolen. Of the approximately half-dozen charges their computer recorded in the last few hours, I had only made one, which was at the restaurant where we had brunch.

When we were leaving the restaurant, I had simply put the card in my pocket, instead of placing it back in my wallet as I normally would. Then, either when I got out of the car to get the paper, or when I took the change out of my pocket to pay for it, the credit card must have fallen out. That was the only stop we made before arriving home. It did not take long for the opportunist who found the card to start treating it as if it were the goose laying the golden eggs.

An encouraging affirmation of the combined effectiveness of modern technology and law enforcement was provided only a few hours after the initial call from the credit card company. Early that evening, I was notified that the police in nearby Fort Lauderdale had arrested the person who was using the card fraudulently. On the down side, nearly two months later, my credit card statement still contained charges that I had clarified at least a couple of times were made by the person who had illegally used my card.

I didn't really need this latest mishap, in the series of mishaps stemming from efforts to procure a Sunday paper, to convince me I should be prioritizing my resources better. But perhaps some readers did, to help acknowledge that the mundane may still be meaningful. For me, this directional coincidence, thrice expressed, brought home the necessity of largely eliminating all extraneous activities not central to writing this book.

The Return of the Warrior

The last coincidence in this section is important because it underscores the commitment and discipline I need to maintain in order to approach this enterprise in the most fruitful manner, as well as the attitude that must be embraced to profit from guidance offered in our everyday world. It is also special to me because it involves the recovery of a small treasure that had been lost for years.

Most mornings my day begins by reading some text dealing with the metaphysical foundation of reality and the most fruitful manner of aligning myself with it. Although this has for decades been the primary subject of the books I read, I am now seeking perspectives that help provide the metaphysical basis of coincidence.

For a while, my mornings began with a book on the fourteenth-century Christian mystic and intellectual Meister Eckhart. The first time I read the twenty-eight sermons the book presents, I was struck by how closely Meister Eckhart's expression of our most fruitful relationship with God is in harmony with the mystical apprehensions of the East. Primarily for that reason, I had decided to review one each morning.

The central point of the talk I read that morning was the effectiveness of relinquishing the calculating ego and limited intellect, to open ourselves up to God's omniscient awareness of the particular things that will serve each of us best. Meister Eckhart related the instruction that one of the first great Christian mystics, St. Dionysius, gave to his students.

St Dionysius was asked by his disciples how it was that one of them, Timothy, outstripped the rest in perfection.

"Dionysius replied; 'Timothy is a man who is passive to God. He who is skilled in this will outstrip all men.'" Meister Eckhart went on to add, "In this sense, your ignorance is not a fault but your chief virtue and your passivity is the chief of your actions. In view of this, you ought to put an end to all your efforts, silence all your faculties, and then you will really discover this birth [of God's Son] in yourself." (Blakney 1941,108)

My coincidence occurred when I got up to get a Bible to review the beatitudes Jesus articulated in the Sermon on the Mount. The precise words of the first beatitude, "Blessed are the poor in spirt for theirs is the kingdom of heaven," was the source of my curiosity, for it encouraged the same posture that Dionysius and Meister Eckhart recommended.

At first glance, being poor in spirit, passive, and ignorant, sounds like strange advice. However, the type of spirit referred to is the type meant when someone is said to be high-spirited and head-strong, which is the sense of being strong-willed and difficult to control. Being willful and head-strong while pursuing our own personally calculated plans and schemes is what is discouraged. Remaining passive and ceasing willful efforts allows God's omniscience to guide us.

This is the same message that was conveyed by the directional coincidence of the meager plums in conjunction with my intended presentation on the *Tao Te Ching* in graduate school. The lesson of that coincidence—have the humility and wisdom to allow the *Tao* (the Divine) unfettered operation in oneself—is crucial for maximizing the benefit of directional coincidences. The passivity that Dionysius and Meister Eckhart advocate reflects the same recognition: the good sense of allowing this unbounded intelligence to guide us, rather than relying on our own clouded view of what we *need* for happiness.

The coincidence occurred in front of the bookshelves from which I had removed my Bible. I was standing barefooted on a very thick rug from northern Africa. The pile of the rug consists of two-inch-long strands of heavy, wool yarn, woven at one end into the matting. The rug is a rich dark brown, like the earth, and as I look back, standing on it in my bare feet was somewhat like being barefoot in a new-plowed field, with the soft earth pressing up between my toes. I mention that because this coincidence has some marked similarities to the earlier coincidence of finding the arrowhead in my garden in Connecticut.

As I was putting the Bible back on the shelf, after standing there briefly referring to it, my toes came down upon something lying on the soft rug. When I bent down to pick it up, I was very surprised, and pleased, to find it was a long-lost artifact I had purchased in Phoenix over a dozen years ago. It was made by the Native American artisan from whom I purchased it. It is a silver ear band with a silver feather hanging down from it. There is a round turquoise stone affixed to the ear band, and another smaller one on the feather.

It is worn by slipping the band over the ear from above, to fit snugly in place about the perimeter of the vertical portion of the ear. I had purchased it before earrings for men were a fad, because the artisan who crafted it told me it was for the warrior. I only intended to wear it when walking or running through the fields and forests of western Connecticut.

I had not seen the ear band for years, until I discovered it beneath my toes. I must have once placed it on top of that Bible, which I had received as a child from Sunday school. Then, at some point, it must have fallen into the ample space between the binding and the pseudo-leather cover, to remain there through a move or two of residence and various references to the Bible. It finally reappeared by falling to the thick brown carpet when I opened the Bible, stimulated by Meister Eckhart's observation that our blessedness and happiness are attained by being passive to God's will.

The coincidence of recovering the long lost warrior's ear band when I sought amplification of Eckhart's words is reinforcement of the warrior posture I had embraced to maximize the potential of successfully writing this book. The marshaling of personal resources, and the discipline and focus required for this endeavor have been like a rebirth of my warriorship.

Although I have experienced numerous coincidences over the last quarter of a century encouraging the disciplined stance of the warrior, the last time I truly marshaled all my resources to become fully disciplined and focused on an enterprise, was probably as a sophomore in high school intent on becoming the first-string fullback on the football team.

There have been a lot of years in between in which I recognized the need, but still did not fully embrace the warrior—until now. If nothing else, I have finally allowed myself to be *passive to God's will*, while committing my whole being to becoming the purest and most effective implement to convey the truths contained here.

After much intermittent pecking at the egg to get out, I have at least at last attained the rebirth of the warrior. The coincidence of the reappearance of the silver and turquoise feathered band from Phoenix, when Eckhart's words stimulated me to refer to the Bible, presented twofold encouragement: it reinforced my own warriorship, as well as the deference to God's will that Eckhart advocates. The latter supplies the ability to profit from directional coincidences, which I am attempting to accomplish in undertaking this enterprise.

This coincidence also provides an illustration of a point cited earlier: the subtleties of a directional coincidence should be treated as potentially meaningful. Previously, we saw how the monk in Korea was not only central to the coincidence I experienced with him, but even his attire, as contrasted to mine, conveyed meaning. Although I was the military man, he was the one in uniform and the one who more fully personified the warrior.

In the coincidence related here, you would need to see and feel between your toes, the long, thick, dark brown strands of the rug, to appreciate how much it resembles the earth of a plowed field— such as the plowed field in which the "More Treasure Unearthed" coincidence revealed the arrowhead that was another symbol of my warriorship.

I am inclined to view this similarity between the two coincidences—of the rug to tilled earth, and of the warrior's ear band to the warrior's arrowhead—as not being accidental. I believe it is likely a connection was being made and a reinforcement of earlier guidance. The difference is that now I am fully complying with the direction provided, in order to maximize the prospect of success.

THE *I CHING* AS DIRECTIONAL COINCIDENCE

The *I Ching* is a classic Chinese book of philosophy and divination that provides the philosophical foundation for both Taoism and Confucianism. The *I Ching*, which may be translated as "The Classic of Flowing Change," perceives change, in concert with the patterns and cycles that govern it, to be the constant of our phenomenological world. Also, for at least four thousand years, the *I Ching* has been used in China as a means of divination—as a kind of forced directional coincidence—to determine if a particular course of action will be beneficial.

The authors of the *I Ching* concluded change was constant and flowed in a cyclical fashion that could be predicted. They realized that, to be successful in their endeavors, it was necessary to anticipate change and to be in harmony with the cycles of change.

David Bohm, a theoretical physicist and associate of Einstein's at Princeton University, underscored the importance some place on change. In his book *Wholeness and the Implicate Order*, Bohm likened the universe to a hologram—a perspective that will be discussed later. The third chapter of his book is entitled "Reality and Knowledge Considered as Process." There, what Bohm calls "process" is the change that is the subject of the *I Ching*:

> The notion that reality is to be understood as process is an ancient one, going back at least to Heraclitus, who said that everything flows. In more modern times, Whitehead was the first to give this notion a systematic and extensive development. . . . I regard the essence of the notion of process as given by the statement: Not only is everything changing, but all is flux. That is to say, what is is the process of becoming itself, while all objects, events, entities, conditions, structures, etc., are forms that can be abstracted from this process.
>
> The best image of process is perhaps that of the flowing stream, whose substance is never the same. On this stream, one may see an ever-changing pattern of vortices, ripples, waves, splashes, etc., which evidently have no independent existence as such. Rather, they are abstracted from the flowing movement, arising and vanishing in the total process of the flow. Such transitory subsistence as may be possessed by these abstracted forms implies only a relative independence or autonomy of behavior, rather than absolutely independent existence as ultimate substances. (Bohm 1980, 48)

So Bohm sees change (process) as being the true reality, and things (no matter what their span of existence) as mere temporary components of that process of change. In the West, the idea that "reality is to be understood as process" may go back only to Heraclitus in the sixth century BCE. But in the East, the more enlightened understanding—that ultimate reality has to do with the principles governing process (change) rather than change itself—has its foundations 1,500 years earlier with the *I Ching*, which is the product of examining those principles. According to the *I Ching*, the key to fruitful activity is to align oneself with those principles, so as to be in harmony with and to profit from change, instead of being uprooted by it.

However, our interest here is in the use for which the *I Ching* was originally intended: as an oracle. The ancient Chinese perceived that change proceeds in cycles that must be accommodated, for to combat them was fruitless. We do not want, metaphorically speaking, to plant vegetables when the earth is frozen. In China, individuals have used the *I Ching* successfully for thousands of years to align themselves with the forces of change currently at play.

The *I Ching* has the capacity to function for us as a kind of forced directional coincidence. The question focused upon when consulting the *I Ching* constitutes the psychological state. The psychophysical event (which is associated with the energized question to form the coincidence) is the hexagram that emerges in the course of consulting the *I Ching*.

The *I Ching* is used by first assigning any three identical coins a numerical value of two for one side and three for the opposite side. The coins are simultaneously tossed while concentrating on a question. The total value of the sides of the three coins that fall face up will be either an odd number ($2 + 2 + 3 = 7$ or $3 + 3 + 3 = 9$), which is represented by an unbroken line (−), or an even number ($3 + 3 + 2 = 8$ or $2 + 2 + 2 = 6$), depicted by a broken line (- -). The coins are tossed six times, and the solid or broken lines resulting from each toss are successively written down to form a six-line figure—the hexagram.

Each of the sixty-four possible hexagrams is representative of some circumstance associated with activity, for example, whether one should proceed in a given situation, in what manner to proceed, the nature of the results if one takes action, what forces or type of individual will be associated with the activity, and so forth. Each possible hexagram has been assigned a number, a name, and a "judgment" that provides further information on the hexagram and the direction in which one should proceed.

Concentrating upon the question in mind while the coins are tossed invests the outcome with mental energy. The particular hexagram that is formed is in essence the coincidence, the psychophysical event corresponding to the psychological state (the energized question).

I feel the rendering by Richard Wilhelm in his book *The I Ching*, which includes a foreword by Carl Jung, remains the best. In that foreword, Jung explains that "the hexagram was understood to be an indicator of the essential situation prevailing in the moment of its origin." Using his term for *coincidence—synchronicity—*he adds:

> Synchronicity takes the coincidence of events in space and time as meaning something more than mere chance, namely, a peculiar interdependence of objective events among themselves as well as with the subjective (psychic) states of the observer or observers. The ancient Chinese mind contemplates the cosmos in a way comparable to that of the modern physicist, who cannot deny that his model of the world is a decidedly psychophysical struc-ture. (Wilhelm 1967, xxiv)

I have used the *I Ching* on and off for well over two decades. In doing so, I have not always received an answer that appeared to be well tailored to the question asked. The *I Ching* itself says that "if one is not as he should be" the oracle will not provide guidance. One needs to be in a calm and receptive state of mind, focused on the question and receptive to direction. These attributes, I might add, are also conducive to directional coincidences.

If one is in a frantic state, with thoughts scattered and leaping about, the possibility of receiving a response that does not address the question appropriately is increased. Or a response that merely reflects one's desires (a mirror coincidence) might occur if one allows oneself to be dominated by a strong desire for a particular type of answer from the *I Ching*.

In the great majority of cases, however, I have found the guid-ance provided to be pertinent to the question asked, especially since I have learned to approach the *I Ching* consistently in the correct psychological posture. In many instances, the answer seemed so specific and well tailored to the question that it appeared as if it were being offered by a compassionate sage in my presence, rather than from a book composed ages ago.

However, there are some other drawbacks and qualifiers regarding use of the *I Ching*, which I will present at the end of this section. In addition, the same guidelines and cautions for employing knowledge gained from analysis of spontaneous coincidences or dreams are also appropriate to applying the guidance provided by the *I Ching*. The wisdom presented by the *I Ching* is but some of the data entered into the cranial computer for the decision-making process. If the judgment seems reasonable and correlates well with known factors, then suitable action may be taken, with continual reevaluation of its appropriateness.

Nearly Split Apart

The wisdom of the *I Ching*, like the guidance provided by directional coincidences, is of little value if it is not complied with, even if it is not what is desired. On occasion, I have not complied with the counsel of the *I Ching*, only to find later that I had no choice but submit to the forces it anticipated.

For example, I had been studying tai chi chuan for a couple of years as an implementation of the principles of Taoism applied to mental and physical health and to self-defense. But I wanted to gain a deeper understanding of the mysterious wisdom of Taoism, especially as expressed in the *Tao Te Ching*. I also wanted to more thoroughly and formally investigate the wisdom expressed in the *I Ching*. My intention was to attain a graduate degree in Chinese philosophy.

The problems were that, as a commercial pilot, I had to fly about four days a week, allocate a three-day weekend twice monthly to be with my sons in Texas, and maintain a large, old colonial home. Maintaining the home required extra attention because I rented a few rooms out to make financial ends meet.

Since graduate school would be a major enterprise, made more difficult by the limitations already imposed upon my time, I decided to see what the *I Ching* had to say about the endeavor. The response was discouraging. The hexagram I received was number twenty-three, which is labeled "Splitting Apart." It consists of five broken (yin) lines beneath one solid (yang) line on top. Since movement or change in the hexagrams is seen to progress from bottom to top, the broken lines in this hexagram are considered to have replaced all the solid lines except the one remaining at the top—the demise of which is near at hand.

Wilhelm offers the following interpretation of this hexagram:

> The lines of the hexagram present the image of a house, the top line being the roof, and because the roof is being shattered the house collapses. The dark lines are about to mount upward and overthrow the last firm, light line by exerting a disintegrating influence on it. The inferior, dark forces overcome what is superior and strong, not by direct means, but by undermining it gradually and imperceptibly, so that it finally collapses.
>
> [This hexagram's judgment is] Splitting Apart. It does not further one to go anywhere.... Under these circumstances, which are due to the time, it is not favorable for the superior man to undertake anything.... For it is a question not of man's doing but of time conditions, which, according to the laws of heaven, show an alternation of increase and decrease, fullness and emptiness. It is impossible to counteract these conditions of the time. Hence it is not cowardice but wisdom to submit and avoid action. (Wilhelm 1967, 93-4)

Hexagram twenty-three clearly not only discouraged embarking upon such a demanding endeavor, but went further to predict a splitting apart and collapse if the undertaking was not avoided. My reaction—so intent was I upon academic pursuit—was to ignore the counsel provided by the hexagram and press on with my plans.

For the first three semesters, I appeared to be able to counteract the prevailing forces. My grades were quite acceptable, and I was able to fulfill my other obligations. I would attend classes five mornings a week, then fly in the afternoon and evening on four of those days. My weekend commitments were also maintained. However, needed maintenance on my home was pretty much ignored, with little prospect of attending to it in the foreseeable future.

Then we pilots agreed to take a twenty percent pay cut to help bolster our airline's financial situation. Consequently, I had to move up to a larger, higher-paying aircraft to help make up the difference in pay. The problem was that the difference in the flight schedule of the new airplane would make it much more difficult for me to attend classes regularly. Next, a great deal of work on an important paper was lost when my computer mysteriously swallowed all the data. Being a novice, I had not saved it on a disk.

It appeared that it was time to consult the *I Ching* again. When I asked about graduate school the second time, I received the exact hexagram that I previously ignored. Now I could no longer ignore it. Knowing that the home symbolizes the individual in dreams, coincidences, and the like, I easily related to the counsel offered: "the lines of the hexagram present the image of a house, the top line being the roof, and because the roof is being shattered the house collapses."

Commencing a new semester with all the demands on my time made it clear that the counsel of the *I Ching* was correct. To embark on a new semester would be to invite a collapse of the home that is my physical and psychological self, from the burden and strain placed upon it. I reluctantly informed my advisor that I would not be continuing my studies, then I took out a home improvement loan to attend to some needed improvements on my actual home, one of the first priorities being a new roof.

What are the chances of receiving the identical hexagram both times, about two years apart, when the same question is asked? More to the point, what are the odds of receiving the exact hexagram that analyzes the situation perfectly both times the question is asked? This is typical of the mysterious ways in which the *I Ching* conveys wisdom.

A Fox Tiptoeing across the Ice

Hexagrams received in connection with writing this book have been very helpful. Earlier I related that I had serious doubts about the correctness of giving up my career, at least temporarily, in order to write this book. To complicate matters, it was not long after I had made that decision that I was encouraged to take advantage of an attractive opportunity to resume work as an airline captain in a part of the country that appealed to me. I decided to consult the *I Ching* with an open heart, to inquire whether my current plans were responsible and correct or whether I should take the safe path of resuming my previous career. The hexagram received was the final one of the book, number sixty-four, entitled "Before Completion."

Wilhelm has the following to say about "Before Completion": "This hexagram indicates a time when the transition from disorder to order is not yet completed. The change is indeed prepared for, since all the lines in the upper trigram are in relation to those in the lower." This hexagram presents the analogy of a fox crossing a river on a thin layer of ice. The fox must be very alert and cautious if it is to successfully reach the other shore. The judgment reads:

> Before completion. Success.
> But if the little fox,
> after nearly completing the crossing,
> Gets his tail in the water,
> There is nothing that would further.

Wilhelm continues: "The conditions are difficult. The task is great and full of responsibility. . . . But it is a task that promises success, because there is a goal that can unite the forces now tending in different directions. At first, however, one must move warily, like an old fox walking over ice" (Wilhelm 1967, 248–249).

The crossing of the river is intended to symbolize the process of making a major transition to a new situation, the far shore of the river. In ancient China, there were few bridges, so crossing a river was a major feat. The fox falling in the water represents the consequences of being distracted and not focusing on the central task that allows attainment of the objective. For me, returning to flying would be a distraction, a divergence that would derail the process of successfully attaining the objective I had set for myself. That objective had, in many ways, entailed a "transition from disorder to order" in my life. When I consulted the *I Ching*, the change was not yet completed, although indeed prepared for. Certainly, the conditions were difficult and the task held much responsibility. Thus, I was relieved to read that, if I remained focused on the goal, the task "promises success."

This hexagram solidified the decision to work on my writing full-time, fully focused. There have been subsequent doubts, but in part because of the support of the *I Ching*, they were less frequent and less debilitating.

Books with Brains

Other encouragement from the *I Ching* occurred unexpectedly in a local bookstore. While there, I noticed a new, very large, almost encyclopedic volume of the *I Ching*. When I opened the book, I was impressed with the detailed presentation on the hexagram before me and also by the fact that it appeared quite relevant in a positive sense to the task in which I was engaged. I wondered if my randomly opening the book to that hexagram was a directional coincidence and whether I might get the same hexagram (number twenty-six) if I consulted the *I Ching* when I returned home. However, once home, I was content with merely reading what was said about the hexagram in one of my editions.

A week later, when I decided to consult the *I Ching* for the first time in quite some time, it was without any particular question in mind, but just to see what wisdom would be conveyed. I had forgotten about the incident in the bookstore until the last line of the hexagram was cast. It was then that I realized it was again number twenty-six, "Nurturance of the Great," which consists of the trigram for heaven beneath the trigram for mountain. The "heaven within the mountain" imagery symbolizes the Divine within humankind. The mountain in its shape, stillness, and solidity conveys the image of a silent individual solidly sitting cross-legged in meditation. The "Nurturance of the Great" that the hexagram encourages, which is facilitated by meditation, is the nurturance of the Divine at the heart of humankind.

The amplification of the hexagram emphasizes holding firm (as a mountain is firm) to one's course while relying on the strong, creative power of heaven for the presentation of truth. Good fortune will result from serving public interests, where even great and difficult undertakings will succeed. In fact, directional coincidences are precisely about relying on the creative power of the Divine, and serving the interests of those who read it is certainly the intent of this book. So, after encountering the same hexagram twice in succession, I took the encounters to be meaningful and its guidance to be pertinent.

Now and then, I will open a book at random and encounter such a directional coincidence, one in which guidance is presented on some situation that is a focus of concern. A fairly recent incident stands out. It does so, in part, because earlier that day a friend had happened to tell me of one of the same types of coincidences, which her husband had just experienced.

Her husband is a pilot who had been kicking around in the commuter airline ranks for some years, but because of the instability of that business, he had not enjoyed any significant career progression. Finally, he took aggressive measures himself. He quit his company so he could enroll in a course to attain an airplane qualification that would enhance his chances of employment with one of the major airlines. He worked very diligently in his course of study, which paid off shortly after he had completed the course. He received a call from the airline that had trained him, requesting that he come for an interview the following day.

That evening, in anticipation of the next day's interview, my friend sat down with a book on the Federal Aviation Regulations (FAR), with which commercial pilots must be familiar. He opened the book at random and began reviewing the regulation before him. The next day, in the interview, he was asked to summarize the exact regulation to which he had spontaneously opened the book. His excellent response was instrumental in the decision of the panel that interviewed him to offer him a position with the company.

A few hours after his wife related this directional coincidence to me over the phone, I had an appointment with a patent attorney. I'd had an idea for a simple invention that would require the expertise of a chemist. When I presented it to a friend who is a chemical engineer, he liked the concept and had a patent search conducted. The patent search presented seventy-four related patents. My friend informed me that he had reviewed them, concluding that none would conflict with a patent application for our product.

The afternoon that we were to initiate the filing of the patent application, the patent attorney was a little late for our appointment. While we waited, I picked up the binder that contained the details of the seventy-four patents on related products and idly opened it at random. I glanced at the particulars of the patent before me, which was filed under a heading that did not suggest any similarity with our product. However, it soon became apparent that it was quite similar. My friend had not noticed the similarity because the title it was filed under gave no hint of a possible conflict with our concept.

If we had filed our patent then, in the manner we intended, it would have no doubt been rejected. Thus, the coincidence of the attorney's tardiness, which allowed the research file to be opened randomly to the only patent that conflicted with ours, provided us with valuable guidance. It saved us from wasting two thousand dollars on an application process that in all likelihood would be denied.

That this type of directional coincidence is genuine and relatively common is highlighted by the fact that, immediately prior to it, my friend related the good fortune her husband had just received in encountering the same type of coincidence. I suspect that nearly everyone reading this account has encountered similar coincidences–those in which a book is randomly opened to the exact page that provides the solution to a problem.

Michael Talbot, in his book *Mysticism and the New Physics*, said that he often consciously employs this type of coincidence to acquire knowledge and with great success. He relates seeking evidence of a common ground that would accommodate both spiritual and scientific perspectives of reality. He thought scientific support would most likely be found in the field of quantum physics. (This was before such works as *The Tao of Physics* and *The Dancing Wu Li Masters* were published.)

He followed up his supposition by going to the physics library of Michigan State University to roam about the vast shelves of books without looking at the myriad titles, waiting for a book to "call" him. After a few minutes, he suddenly felt a compulsion to grab a book from the shelf, which he opened at random. It opened to an article on quantum mechanics and reality, which presented the major conclusions he had arrived at, only approached from a different discipline. It was just what he was hoping to find.

Talbot adds, "I cannot begin to relate how many dozens of people have told me identical stories, accounts of how they walked into a bookstore or library and gravitated mysteriously but unerringly toward precisely the book or article they needed to answer some pressing question" (Talbot 1992, 138).

Certainly, many people perform a similar, although less formal, procedure when browsing in a bookstore. They will pick up a book that could be of interest and open it randomly, to see if the passage they encounter strikes a chord of relevance or provides special meaning. They are sometimes startled by how appropriate the meaning is. My coincidences with the *I Ching* and with the patent search, my friend's coincidence with the FAR, and Michael Talbot's experiences suggest that the next time this happens to you, the information provided should perhaps not be lightly dismissed.

A Word of Caution

Early in this discussion of the *I Ching* as a forced directional coincidence, I mentioned that there are some drawbacks and restrictions to its use in this capacity. That is not to say that it is not a useful instrument for revealing the truth. In fact, as death approached the renowned sage Confucius, he said that his one regret was that he did not have more time remaining to study the *I Ching*. This underscores the great respect this classic has earned throughout the ages in China, until modern rationalism belittled it. But it also points to one of its drawbacks. Even for a sage like Confucius, interpreting the *I Ching* was no easy task. For one thing, the symbolism is frequently subtle and esoteric, and it takes some time to become familiar with it. Even Chinese scholars will have varied interpretations of some aspects of identical hexagrams.

On top of that, we Westerners must refer to translations of material that, even in the original language, are not without error in interpretation and transmission. The problem is compounded by the fact that an incorrect interpretation in a translation is naturally more likely. Even an excellent work, such as the Wilhelm edition, is not without error.[1]

A second difficulty is that the one consulting the *I Ching* may focus on particular aspects of the hexagram received that conform to her or his desires and expectations while the essential meaning, because it is less appealing, is ignored. Even if one has an open mind and attempts to be objective, it is difficult to know which of various aspects are most pertinent, particularly if the interpretation of a moving line is at odds with the general meaning of the hexagram. This, in addition to the aforementioned difficulties of interpreting the symbolism that permeates the work, makes discerning meaning quite challenging.

I already mentioned the condition that "if one is not as he should be" the oracle will not provide guidance. If one's mind is agitated, the hexagram received cannot be relied upon. Furthermore, if a particular type of response (encouragement to proceed in a course of action, for example) is intensely desired, a mirror

---

1. For instance, Wilhelm's *I Ching* titles hexagram twenty-six (cited in *Books with Brains*) "The Taming Power of the Great." This is both inconsistent with the symbolism inherent in the two trigrams comprising the hexagram and at odds with the perspective of other scholars. "The Power of Taming the Great" would have been a correct title, in harmony with both the symbolism and the interpretation of other scholars. The hexagram depicts *heaven* beneath, and thus within, the *mountain*–the latter symbolizing a person sitting cross-legged in meditation, who in his shape and his stillness resembles a mountain. The heaven within the person/mountain is then the soul or spirituality, which is accumulated, nurtured, stored up, restrained, tamed, etc., within the person who has stilled his or her mind. Thus the hexagram may be correctly perceived to depict a "Nurturance of the Great," as Thomas Cleary depicts it in *The Taoist I Ching* (Boston: Shambhala Publications, 1986, 115), a "storing up" or "accumulation of virtue," as James Legge (*continued overleaf*)

coincidence in which that desire is reflected by a hexagram may result, instead of valid guidance by the *I Ching* as directional coincidence.

But beyond restrictions imposed by the fact that one must be focused, calm, receptive, respectful, even reverent, the ability to force the *I Ching* to provide a directional coincidence has another limitation. Even a very correct attitude when consulting the *I Ching* provides no guarantee that a reply will be received that accurately conveys an impending course of events. There are some things about our futures that we simply are not supposed to know in advance.

For example, I have on two occasions asked about important, quite different situations I was contemplating, and both times I received the hexagram entitled "Difficulty at the Beginning." The judgment reads, "Difficulty at the beginning works supreme success," conveying the idea of the difficulty of a new birth and the growth pains that are preconditions of the strength and vitality of maturity. Yet in both cases, the difficulties encountered in the beginning persisted throughout the duration of the situations.

My conclusion is that I was supposed to experience those situations as requisites for growth. I was led to believe that in each I would eventually find "supreme success," when in reality this did not happen. However, in both cases, experiencing the circumstances did allow for the realization of success later on, elsewhere.

---

interprets it (*I Ching Book of Changes* (University Books, 1964, 113), an "Accumulation Through Restraint," as Alfred Douglas labels it (*How to Consult The I Ching* (New York: G.P. Putnam's Sons, 1971, 125), or "The Power of Taming the Great," which the Wilhelm edition mistranslates as "The Taming Power of the Great." Wilhelm even states: "The Creative (heaven) is tamed by Kên (mountain), Keeping Still. This produces great power"—which clearly is the "power of taming the great" by the attributes of the mountain, and not "the taming power of the great." Suffice it to say that this illustrates the pitfalls of using a translation of a difficult text, particularly one that, in the original language finds varied and sometimes conflicting interpretation. Actually, the English version of Wilhelm's *I Ching* is a translation of a translation. It is quite possible errors such as the one above were not committed by Wilhelm, but by C. F. Baynes, who translated Wilhelm's German into English.

I've also encountered a number of instances in which the *I Ching* provided oblique answers in response to important questions. The truth of the answers was difficult to perceive until the situation was already concluded and could be viewed retrospectively. That is not to say that someone more sagacious and perspicacious could not have deciphered the meaning before the circumstances unfolded about him. But if you are a person of average intelligence, like myself, stumbling along trying to read the road map correctly, the *I Ching* can throw you some sliders and knuckleballs with which it is difficult to make good contact.

IN SUMMARY

These difficulties with the use of the *I Ching* underscore the reasons that directional coincidences, which are unforced and spontaneous, can be of such value. The limitation of not being able to invoke a directional coincidence on demand may actually be viewed as an asset.

We are provided with the particular instruction that is appropriate for us, as determined by a level of genius that far surpasses our own. The decision of what we need to know and when we need to know it may be better left to a higher authority. In like manner, if you or I wanted to become a surgeon, we would not want to be put in the position of determining the order and content of our curriculum. We would much prefer that those decisions were in the more capable hands of someone who already possessed the full knowledge and wisdom that the course of study ultimately makes accessible.

If we truly open ourselves up to divine guidance, we do not need to worry about what must be known and what course of activity must be pursued. We simply relinquish the responsibility for those determinations to the Divine. As Meister Eckhart observes of God, "In all his gifts, he gives himself to the limit of the capacity of him who is to receive" (Blakney 1941, 220). We must simply open ourselves up to the ample guidance that will be provided by the directional coincidences encountered in this classroom of life. Then we will each be supplied with knowledge and wisdom appropriate to our particular abilities to receive and apply it. We will, in this way, be gently led forward on our quest for the currents of that river of contentment and bliss we all seek.

Again (in contrast with the esoteric symbolism of the *I Ching*), we will not be provided with guidance that is beyond our capacity to appreciate. What is the point of furnishing a directional coincidence if one cannot understand the direction? That is not to say that we will not have to stretch a bit and exercise our powers of inquiry. But the challenge is part of what makes it entertaining. Who wants to play a game in which one wins simply by showing up?

The observations I have put forth in this chapter about directional coincidences need not be accepted without reservation, but it is important not to dismiss them outright. They simply need to be put to the test, to be evaluated openly for truth and effectiveness.

Keeping a coincidence journal is probably the best way to put the meaningfulness of coincidences and the appropriateness of your interpretations to the test. You can write down the coincidence and a tentative interpretation of meaning to see whether the flow of events verifies or denies your interpretation. If meaning is not clear initially, the coincidence may simply be recorded in anticipation that its significance may be revealed later. With this method, you have a record that allows for a more or less scientific evaluation of meaningfulness over an extended period of time.

Cymbals and Symbols

WE BEGAN THE INTRODUCTION with a quote from Forrest Gump. Perhaps we might profit by paying him another visit. Remember the feather that was floating around in the beginning of the movie, and at the end too? It was obviously there for a reason. Most of us have some sense of the feather's meaning, even if we can not state it exactly.

Clearly, the feather is a symbol. The feather symbolizes Forrest Gump: Forrest Gump the individual as well as *Forrest Gump* the movie. No matter where the breeze blows that feather—up, down, back, and forth—the feather does only one thing: it just floats along without resistance, simply being itself, a feather floating in the breeze. No matter which way the winds of fate blow Forrest, he does just one thing, which is to be true to himself, to be just plain Forrest. He always remains—through the worst of times and the best of times— loving, simple, compassionate, committed, humble, and generous. That is why we love him.

The feather symbolizes a bit more than that (which we will touch upon a little later). But in its most immediate meaning, it represents that quality of remaining "simply Forrest," no matter what forces buffet him.

His integrity, his ability to remain true to himself while simply accepting the forces of life (and death) that propel him along his path is his greatness. It is what endears him to us. And it is in large part what the movie is all about. This posture, which Forrest naturally adheres to, happens to be necessary to profit from the directional coincidences that are at the heart of this book—with one added ingredient. We are encouraged to attend to the breezes that blow us about, so that we may use them to navigate our serendipitous journey. Actually, Forrest is not so bad at that, either.

In this chapter, we are going to explore the simple and logical methods that may be used to analyze symbols such as Forrest's feather. We do this with good reason. As we have seen, coincidental events are frequently symbolic. Yet the method shown here is not exclusive to coincidences. It works wherever we encounter symbols: in dreams, myths, poems, art, literature, movies—the world at large.

UNIVERSAL SYMBOLS

We know that a symbol is something that spontaneously, in uncontrived manner, represents another thing, quality, emotion—something that conveys meaning beyond its obvious and immediate surface meaning. With many symbols, we have a direct and immediate recognition of meaning, in both the unconscious and conscious mind. Anyone listening to Richard Wagner's *The Ride of the Valkyries*, upon hearing the cymbals clash, knows what the cymbals symbolize. Without being told, we know that the resounding clash of the cymbals in any musical work represents something dramatic, frequently a climax of some sort. The sound of cymbals spontaneously evokes the same feelings and images in everyone everywhere.

As we have seen in previous examples, this is a universal symbol. In chapter one, a universal symbol was identified as one that is experienced the same—has the same meaning—for virtually everyone. A universal symbol is usually experienced the same in various cultures all over the world. However, it may only be universal to a particular culture while not known, or not experienced the same, in other parts of the world.

So direct and immediate is the symbolic meaning of cymbals clashing that we do not need to stop and analyze what is being conveyed. Yet with many universal symbols (though we may have a spontaneous, intuitive sense of meaning) our recognition may remain primarily beneath the conscious level of awareness. Thus, if we were asked to state explicitly the symbol's significance, we would have difficulty doing so. That is why we need to familiarize ourselves with how to analyze symbols.

The first step in determining meaning is to establish the symbol's essential qualities and function. When we speak of the essential qualities and function, this is in the subjective context of how we each experience or view it. A shark is basically an animal that lives in the ocean. Yet, since the quality we essentially associate it with is that of a ruthless, tenacious, deadly predator, that is quite likely what it symbolizes to us.

Although most will have little difficulty recognizing the meaning of the symbol in the following example, analyzing it according to its essential qualities and functions will help us become familiar with the way that is accomplished. And we will also see how the specific meaning of a symbol in a particular situation is dependent upon the context in which it is used.

Say it is a dark, cloudy day in Seattle—not that I am trying to imply there are a lot of cloudy days there. It's just that all day long on this dark and cloudy day in Seattle, an architect has been unsuccessfully seeking the solution to a problem in a major project. Finally, late in the day, after she has nearly given up on resolving the difficulty, a brilliant solution pops into her head. Immediately, she knows it is the one perfect answer. At that exact moment— for the first time all day—out over Puget Sound, the sun suddenly bursts through a hole in the dark clouds, to send its bright rays streaming in through her tenth-floor window.

Here is a mirror coincidence in which the coincidental event is symbolic. From what we know about mirror coincidences, we can see that the great amount of psychic energy that was invested in seeking a solution to the problem, which reached its peak when the solution emerged, was correlated with the coincidental event of the sun just then breaking through the clouds.

Fortunately, the sun is not only about as universal as a symbol may be, but its meaning is also quite easy to perceive, especially its specific meaning relative to this hypothetical coincidence. But just for the exercise, let's go through the normal steps for clarifying potential meanings of the symbol. Again, this same process works equally well in analyzing symbols contained in dreams and other vehicles of expression.

The first step has been accomplished. We know the sun is a universal rather than personal symbol. The next step is to identify its essential nature, qualities, or functions. We are interested in how we experience and view the symbol, rather than its objective qualities. It is little help to acknowledge that the sun is a star with a diameter of 864,000 miles, a mass 333,000 times that of the earth, and that it is 93,000,000 miles away. That says nothing of how we relate to it—its meaning for us.

We most immediately relate to the sun as that which provides light and warmth. Light, or illumination, symbolizes awareness or knowledge. That is why we intuitively know that a phrase such as "I've seen the light" means "I understand." Warmth symbolizes to us the warmth of affection or love, such as is conveyed by identifying someone as a person of real warmth. So we may conclude the basic symbolic meanings of the sun are, on the one hand, knowledge or awareness, and on the other, love or the warmth of affection. In addition, since the light and warmth of the sun make us feel good, we associate happiness and cheerfulness with the sun as well, such as when we describe someone as having a sunny disposition.

On a deeper level, the sun's properties have always presented humankind with a more profound symbol. While it possesses and bestows illumination and warmth, it also brings about new life and the rejuvenation of the old with the coming of every spring. Although it may be hidden from view, we know it will not abandon us, for we are sure that on the morn it will rise again. As such, it is experienced as eternal. Its abode is the heavens, which it dominates. It is unbounded, and its influence (its rays) extends over vast reaches. All these together have throughout time, for cultures around the globe, rendered the sun a symbol of the Divine.

Usually, as in the example we are investigating, we need to do more than merely determine the general meaning of a symbol. We need to take a look at the context in which the symbol appears, for this reveals more specific meaning. For instance, a sunrise, in being associated with the dawning of a new day, symbolizes a new beginning, a fresh start, a new era. A setting sun, in occurring at the end of the day, may symbolize the end of a cycle, such as the end of life or of prosperity.

In the coincidence presented above, the sudden awareness of the solution by the architect is the context in which the sun appears, as is the simultaneous, sudden penetration of the dark clouds by the sun to provide sudden illumination. Thus, sudden illumination (coinciding with the sudden solution) is the specific symbolic meaning of the sun in the context of the coincidental circumstances.

Coincidentally, here in Coconut Grove, Florida, it was cloudy all day with frequent rain when I first wrote about the architect's solution accompanied by the sudden burst of sunlight. It was a welcome change, after five days of sunshine, to watch the raindrops refresh the lush vegetation outside my window.

I had quite a bit of difficulty working out how to present the hypothetical coincidence most effectively. When I finally finished, I decided to step outside for a breath of fresh air. A moment or two after I was outside, I realized my small backyard was bathed in sunlight. I looked up to see the pronounced border of a mass of dark clouds, which had just receded enough to reveal the bright sun and blue sky for the first time all day. A smile came to my face as I realized that here was an actual coincidence that mirrored the hypothetical one I had just completed writing about.

This was not an especially important or dramatic coincidence. It was merely one of those interesting incidents that occur once we open up to the coincidences happening around us. Here again, coincidences are similar to dreams. Many have observed that, when you start paying attention to dreams, you seem to have both more dreams and more revealing dreams.

A Refrigerator in Heaven

In contrast to the sun, is a refrigerator a universal symbol? In developed countries everywhere, the essential quality or function of a refrigerator is the same. Anything that is experienced or viewed similarly by much of humanity qualifies as a universal symbol.

I mention a refrigerator because one was central to the last coincidence in chapter one, in which the woman who bought a refrigerator my mother had advertised for sale had previously worked for my mother's cousin in a town three thousand miles away. To determine the meaning of that coincidence, let's try to discover the symbolic value of a refrigerator.

Sometimes the shape of an object may play a part in what it symbolizes, which is true of the shape of a pearl, for instance. However, with a refrigerator, we may think it is safe to assume its form is not particularly significant. What are the first things that come to mind when you think of a refrigerator? I think of its function, which is to preserve food, and with that comes the idea of keeping the food fresh. I also think of it as being cold inside. And, like my mother's refrigerator, I envision a refrigerator as being white.

It is fascinating to see how symbols spontaneously manifest meaning. When I first thought about the potential symbolic meanings of a refrigerator, I had a vague idea of how one quality might be pertinent to my mother's coincidence. Then, as I finished identifying the various essential qualities of a refrigerator, I was surprised to see how—one after another—each potential meaning of this symbol was dramatically related to the coincidence. Even its shape, which I had initially discounted as being irrelevant to meaning, proves to be meaningful.

Let us begin by examining the first quality mentioned: the refrigerator's essential function of preserving food. When I reflected on whether that function might be relevant to the coincidence, it occurred to me that my mother's cousin's daughter had, previous to the coincidence, compiled a family tree for that side of the family, which had emigrated from Denmark. A family tree preserves one's heritage and one's identity. I felt there was a fair chance that the shared function of the refrigerator and the family tree, of preserving, provided the refrigerator with the symbolic meaning pertinent to this coincidence and was the connection here between my mother and her cousin in California.

Next, it occurred to me that, if this was a mirror coincidence, a charged complex should be involved. When I pondered what it might be, I suddenly recalled that my mother's second husband had died shortly before she replaced the refrigerator. In fact, that is why she was selling the refrigerator. She felt she no longer needed one that large for just herself, thus was replacing it with a smaller one.

So here was the charged complex: the death complex. The refrigerator was associated with my mother's energized death complex, for it was because of her husband's death that she was selling the refrigerator in the first place. In addition, the ensuing heightened perception of her mortality prompted the wish that her identity be preserved. This was symbolized by the family tree compiled by her cousin's daughter and also by the refrigerator in its different capacity to preserve.

The refrigerator not only symbolizes preserving one's identity after death because of its function, but also in regard to the quality I had initially dismissed: its shape, which is that of a coffin. It also symbolizes a coffin due to its previously mentioned function of preserving. Just as a refrigerator serves to preserve, the coffin preserves one's remains.

Another essential quality of a refrigerator, that of keeping things cold, is also here associated with death and with a coffin. When the body dies, it becomes cold. The contents of both a refrigerator and a coffin are markedly cold.

Finally, there is the factor of color. White is the standard color of refrigerators, and it was the color of my mother's refrigerator. White is associated with purity and a sterile environment, such as a hospital. Yet here again we encounter a symbol that is associated with death, for in this instance, white symbolizes heaven. We have just noted that, in both its shape and in its function to preserve, a refrigerator may be symbolic of a coffin. Similarly, here it is in both its color (white) and its capacity to keep things free from bacteria that it is associated with purity and sterility, thus with heaven.

For my mother, though, it is not so much the pure and sterile aspect of white that symbolizes heaven. It is a twist on the primary meaning of sterility that white normally elicits, which for her symbolizes heaven. Here, heaven is sterile in the sense of being the opposite of potent. For her, if by chance there is a heaven, it is a sterile place, not alive and vibrant, but impotent and austere. Furthermore, the idea of heaven is, for her, sterile and impotent. Although my mother is a regular churchgoer, she believes that when we die—that's it! The only thing that is preserved is our legacy: our record of existence (family tree), our children, and our children's children. To her, the idea of a heaven (and heaven itself if it does exist) is cold and sterile, like a refrigerator is cold and sterile.

There is one last analogy in this coincidence that we now recognize to be a classic mirror coincidence. It is another analogy between the refrigerator and my mother's death complex. This last essential component of the coincidence reinforced something I already knew about my mother: She is both practical and courageous. She does not excessively fear the prospect of death. She has prepared herself for it. This is symbolized by the very act that precipitated the coincidence, for how many people would take the trouble to replace a perfectly good refrigerator with one that is smaller?

The large refrigerator, in both shape and function, symbolized (among other things) a coffin for the large man who was her husband. She replaced it with a smaller refrigerator (a symbolic coffin that is more her size) in anticipation, preparation, and acceptance of her journey's eventual end. This clearly symbolizes her coming to terms with her own mortality. Nevertheless, it does stimulate strong feelings in the charged death complex, and she does want a legacy to remain, symbolized by the ongoing family tree compiled by her cousin's daughter.

I must admit I am surprised at how the many symbolic meanings of the refrigerator, and the meaning of this mirror coincidence, suddenly unfolded. Yet in many ways, this was a classic example of how symbols function in both dreams and coincidences and how meaning can be determined. We can see how the particular context in which universal symbols are used provides specific tones and hues to the symbol's meaning.

We have also seen how knowledge of factors in an individual's life situation may be vital to determining, or substantiating, which meanings of a symbol are specifically relevant. This is a key element that must be considered whenever that information is available. The psychological factors that are heightened for the protagonist at the time a symbol materializes are extremely important clues to its meaning.

We have noted the creative and liberal way in which a quality of a symbol, or a word representing a quality, may be used. We should be receptive to the widest range of possible meanings in the process of determining specific meaning for the case in question. Recall the various ways in which the concept to preserve was appropriate in this coincidence.

A word representing a particular meaning of a symbol may also be used to convey a different meaning of that word. This was illustrated by the fact that the whiteness and function of the refrigerator, representing a sterile environment in the sense of being free of germs, actually symbolized for my mother a different but somewhat related connotation of the word *sterile*, in the sense of being impotent. Such gymnastics are common with symbols, so again we need to maintain an open, even creative perspective when determining meaning.

It is important to recognize that there are many other ways the essential meanings of this universal symbol could be used in other circumstances. It need not have anything at all to do with death. For instance, if in a dream or coincidence a refrigerator functioned to preserve a wedding corsage or part of a wedding cake, the symbolic significance would be entirely different. One must first identify the essential function and qualities of the symbol, then see if there are factors pertinent to the situation in which the symbol appears and/or pertinent to the protagonist's psychological state, which might highlight one or more of the meanings in a particular way.

The Cup of Life

Let's look at some symbols a great many people in the West are very familiar with: the symbols associated with the Last Supper. The wine as a symbol used in the sacrament of Holy Communion is familiar to all Christians, as well as to much of the rest of the world. Yet the symbolic meaning of the cup that contains the wine is not understood by most and not acknowledged in the dogma of Christianity. The correct interpretation of this important symbol sheds new light on the meaning of the crucifixion. The circumstances surrounding the Last Supper and the crucifixion provide enough information to allow a conclusive, logical analysis of the significance of Jesus' reference to the cup, an analysis that can alter traditional attitudes about the crucifixion and about those held responsible for the death of Jesus.

At the Last Supper, Jesus "took the cup, and gave thanks, and gave it to them, saying, Drink ye all of it; For this is my blood of the new testament" (Matthew 26:27-28).[1] Let's first look at the essential quality and function of the wine/blood as it relates to the Last Supper. We know the wine symbolizes the blood, for this is explicitly stated. Indeed, both wine and blood are red. They are also both fluids. And the wine is the fermented essence of the grape, just as blood is the essence of the body. But when Jesus tells his disciples to drink all of his blood, he obviously does not mean that literally. Therefore, the blood must symbolize something else.

Just as blood is the fluid physical essence of the body, without which the body would perish, there is a truer essence without which the physical being would perish. This is that which enlivens the body: the spirit. No matter what religion we subscribe to, if any, we all believe that, when the spirit departs, the body dies, just as it will succumb when the blood has flowed out.

In a different sense, we associate the reddening of the complexion when the blood rushes to the surface of the skin with being in a spirited state: of excitement, anger, or other strong emotion. Here again, blood and spirit are linked.

However, the meaning of the cup is more provocative than the wine. A cup is referred to twice in short succession in poignant circumstances just prior to the crucifixion. First, during the Last Supper, "he took the cup, and gave thanks, and gave it to them, saying to them, Drink ye all of it" (Matthew 26:27). Then, imme-

---

1. All quotations from the Bible used in this word are taken from the King James Version, unless otherwise noted.

diately afterward, at the Mount of Olives (Gethsemane), "he was withdrawn from them about a stone's cast, and kneeled down, and prayed, Saying, Father, if thou be willing, take this cup from me; nevertheless not my will, but thine, be done" (Luke 22:42).

First, Jesus took the cup and gave thanks and gave it to his disciples, commanding them to drink all of its contents; in the next situation, we are told he asked God to take the cup from him. What is the cup that he refers to? What does the cup symbolize? In the first instance, we know that when Jesus took the cup and said "drink ye all of it for this is my blood," he is saying to his disciples, "take and embrace the Spirit of Christ, the Holy Spirit, fully and completely." For we know the wine represents the blood, which symbolizes the spirit.

The cup must then symbolize that which in reality contains Jesus' blood and spirit. In a different sense from the bread that is shared in the Last Supper,[2] clearly, the cup symbolizes Jesus' body, which contains and, in his case, confines his spirit. When Jesus asks God to "take this cup from me," he is clearly asking God to relieve him of that which contains and confines his spirit, to relieve him of his body.

Not only must Jesus be crucified to fulfill biblical prophecy, he specifically asks God to take his body, if that is in accord with God's will ("yet not my will, but thine, be done"). And it obviously is God's will also, for it is done.

Supporting evidence may be found in the common ritual of presenting a toast. In presenting a toast, we may stand or we may merely raise our cup or glass. Both represent the same thing. When we stand we are raising ourselves—containing our spirit—and

---

2. "And as they were eating, Jesus took bread, and blessed it, and broke it, and gave it to the disciples, and said, 'Take, eat; this is my body'" (Matthew 26:26). Jesus blessed the bread just as, by his austerities and devotion to God, he blessed and made sacred his own body: first, in breaking his individual, personal willfulness to align himself with God's will; second, in allowing his body to be broken (given, sacrificed) for the good of his disciples and the rest of Christianity. Like the body, bread is solid and of a particular form, whereas like wine and blood, we consider the spirit of God to be fluid and flowing, not intrinsically confined to form.

offering our "good spirit" to the recipient. When we raise the cup containing the "spirits," we are doing the same thing, for the raised cup symbolizes our physical self and the spirits it contains—our own good spirits and our spirited support and recognition.

This symbolic recognition of meaning is not mysterious or esoteric, but straightforward, logical, and clear. We know that the way to substantiate or discredit an interpretation of symbolic meaning is to see if the circumstances surrounding the symbol's use reinforce the interpretation. In this case, the circumstances fully corroborate the interpretation that when Jesus asks God to "take this cup from me," he is asking God to "take this body from me."

Jesus repeatedly reveals that he knows exactly what will happen to him, yet he makes no effort at all to alter the course of events and escape the impending crucifixion. Four times before the Last Supper, Jesus foretells his death. Then, during the Last Supper, he states that it will, in fact, be his last supper. He says Peter will deny him three times before the cock crows. He states that Judas will betray him; it is as if Jesus instructs Judas to betray him. He welcomes with compassion those who have come to take him into custody, without anger or any avoidance (he even heals the soldier's ear that was sliced off by a zealous follower). Jesus knows all that will happen, yet he makes no effort at all to alter or avoid the course of events.

Even at his trial before Pontius Pilate, Jesus makes not the slightest effort to defend himself. Then at Calgary, on the cross, Jesus responds to the plea of one of the two crucified with him, saying, "Verily I say unto thee, today shalt thou be with me in paradise" (Luke 23:43). He does not express remorse, but looks forward to entering paradise. Yet after this, even for Jesus, a period of doubt occurs, which is symbolized by the descent of darkness: "And it was about the sixth hour, and there was a darkness over all the earth until the ninth hour. And the sun was darkened, and the veil of the temple was rent in the midst" (Luke 23:44–45). As we know, light symbolizes awareness or knowledge, including spiritual illumination. Darkness here, of course, then symbolizes ignorance—a shrouding of knowledge or illumination. And this is apparently what even Jesus suffers. For at the end of the three hours of darkness, he cries out, apparently to God in despair at not having yet been taken, at being both literally and symbolically "left hanging there." He pleads, *"Eloi, Eloi, lama sabachthani?,"* which is being interpreted as "My God, my God, why hast thou forsaken me?" (Mark 15:34).

Yet even here, on the cross in despair, Jesus provides us with a lesson. It is that, in our darkest hour of doubt and misery, if we beseech God with all our being, we will not be denied. For Jesus' plea was followed by the serene expression of his last words: "He said, Father, into thy hands I commend my spirit: and having said thus, he gave up the ghost" (Luke 23:46). Thus, we can see that Jesus is aware that his prayer of despair is being answered and the ordeal is over, when in his final words he says, "Father, into thy hands I commend my spirit."

For an enlightened person, this attitude and conduct toward the surrender of the body are not at all surprising. To an individual who has realized his or her own divinity, the physical body may be a hindrance, or at least something to be transcended, and not clung to. In fact, there are many examples throughout history of enlightened beings willingly relinquishing their body. Since these help to further substantiate our recognition of the meaning of the cup symbolism, let's take a look at a few of them.

For many centuries the great saint of Islam, Mansur al'Hallaj (856–921) has been known in Sufism as the model of one who sacrificed his life for love of God and for truth. In prison one night, he freed all the other prisoners. In the morning, when the jailers asked why he remained, he replied, "A servant must wait at home until his lord comes." Previous to his imprisonment, he prayed to God, "Alas here am I, in the prison of life, reunited with the whole human race . . . Ah, take me with you outside that prison." In a poem he said, "People make the pilgrimage to Mecca; I am going on a pilgrimage to my Host; while they offer animals for sacrifice, I offer my heart and blood." (Levy 1987, 84) Mansur al'Hallaj was ultimately executed for the crime of declaring his oneness with God.

Emanuel Swedenborg provides another example of a saint willing and eager to relinquish the body for what lies beyond. Swedenborg, some of whose accomplishments we will examine in the next chapter, was perhaps the most multifaceted intellectual of eighteenth-century Europe. He made original contributions in over a dozen scientific fields, as well as in philosophy and theology. However, he was most renowned for his powers of extrasensory perception and for his radical Christianity.

Among those Swedenborg calmly informed of the exact date of his coming death was the theologian John Wesley, whom he told in a letter. The great twentieth-century Zen scholar, D. T. Suzuki, so admired Swedenborg that he wrote a book about him, in which he notes the following about Swedenborg's departure:

> He abandoned his earthly body in a London boarding house. He knew of his death beforehand, informing the proprietress and maid. They said that, in watching the approach of his death, Swedenborg was as delighted as a child who was going off to a festival or out to play. During his lifetime, this old man of 84 years had already witnessed conditions in the other world. He had a personal and thorough knowledge of where he would go. So, knowing that he would at last enter this region, why should he not be pleased? (Suzuki 1996, 37)

In the next chapter we'll also become familiar with some of the achievements and metaphysical perceptions of Paramahansa Yogananda. Early in the twentieth century, he was the first great Indian saint to take permanent residence in the United States. He was so well accepted that he was invited to the White House to meet the president, would fill Carnegie Hall for his talks, and still has a large following.

Yogananda was in perfect health in his late fifties when, while meditating in a large hall with many followers, he simply left his body for the last time. The previous day he had expressed pleasure in receiving a fresh coconut from Florida, for he said he wanted to enjoy the taste of coconut one last time, before going on his "great journey."

Not fearing, even relishing the passing from this plane of existence, are more the rule than the exception for those who have realized their own divinity. Thus, it is not the least surprising that Jesus too would welcome leaving his body behind. This is a new way of looking at the crucifixion: as a dramatic statement made by Jesus. His actions may be perceived as a metaphor, that to live for a worthy ideal is of far greater value than the corporeal thing we reside in while here. And if we work toward achieving the potential for goodness we each have within, we may look forward to, rather than fear, what lies beyond this realm.

According to the Christian perspective, the ideal Jesus lived and died for was simply the salvation of humanity. The words of Jesus are eloquent and imbued with the power of truth. But what most sets him apart are his actions, the culmination of which was his crucifixion. For it was his own drama, which he orchestrated in concert with God.

In this investigation, we have taken two symbols–the wine and the cup that held it–and analyzed their meaning according to their essential quality and function in the context in which they appear. We have also substantiated the meaning of the cup with an objective appraisal of the circumstances surrounding its use as a symbol. Additional evidence has been provided by examples of saints who have welcomed their own passing. These are the logical steps we should take to determine the meaning of symbols in coincidences, dreams, or wherever we encounter them.

There is an additional factor in this example that is quite pertinent to the directional coincidences we investigated in the second chapter. It is Jesus' request of God, after he asked that the cup (body) be taken from him, that "not my will, but thy will be done." It is probably commonly thought that Jesus defers to God's will (and earlier, in the Lord's Prayer, urged his followers to do the same) because God is the creator, the ruler, the highest authority, and the one to which we owe our loyalty and obedience. This is true, but there is also another practical reason that Jesus encourages us to do so.

The best source for an explanation may be Meister Eckhart, the fourteenth-century Dominican priest, intellectual, and mystic. The fact that Meister Eckhart is held in very high esteem today is underscored by the numerous books in print about his comprehension of reality, including a recent one entitled *Meister Eckhart: The Man from Whom God Hid Nothing.* Eckhart says the following about aligning ourselves with God's will: "You should know that to those persons who put themselves completely in God's hands, and seek with all diligence to do his will, all that God gives is best of all. Be sure, as God lives, that it is necessarily the best and that nothing could be better" (Blakney 1941, 183).

So the practical consequence of deferring to God's direction is that what each of us receives in return is the very best possible gift. The idea is that God knows what will provide each of us with enduring happiness far better than we do. Yet Meister Eckhart also raises the question: "Now likely, you will ask: 'How shall I know whether it is the will of God or not?' As for that, know that if it were not God's will it could not be" (Blakney 1941, 183).

So if we put ourselves "in God's hands," God will unremittingly provide us with the appropriate guidance for attaining what is "necessarily the best." This is the practical reason for opening ourselves up to directional coincidences and heeding the guidance they provide. It is God's way of leading each of us individually, according to our particular needs, to that which will provide us with enduring contentment.

PERSONAL SYMBOLS

Many of the things we know about universal symbols apply equally well to the other basic type of symbol, the personal symbol. We still need to assess the symbol's basic quality and function, and how the one encountering the symbol experiences or views it. In fact, it is precisely how the symbol is perceived or experienced by the individual encountering it that principally determines the meaning of a personal symbol.

Let us say you have a dream in which you are told to call extension 3211. The next morning, you find the combination to the lock on the supply room at work has been changed to 3211. Later, after contemplating this little coincidence, you recall that your childhood sweetheart lived on 3211 Highridge Road. The meaning would then most likely be related to that relationship, perhaps suggesting that you should contact that person for some reason, or that something learned in that relationship is applicable to a current dilemma. In any case, in this coincidence, 3211 serves as a personal symbol which, for you, represents that relationship.

Even with a universal symbol, the way it is experienced by an individual takes precedence over its common meaning. We saw, in a previous example, how the general meanings of the sun as a universal symbol were less appropriate and informative than the meaning derived by the specific context in which it appeared. The same held true of the refrigerator in my mother's coincidence.

To go a step further, if a universal symbol has been experienced repeatedly, or in a highly charged situation, in a manner peculiar to the protagonist which is different from its universal meaning, it may well function for him or her as a personal symbol with a meaning different from the meaning it has for others. Meaning is then derived from the particular associations it gained in the repetitious or charged situation.

For instance, in the "intense love/painful separation" complex we explored in chapter one, we saw how vintage Mustang convertibles came to symbolize a psychological situation. This association replaced the universal meaning of a car, which, as a personal vehicle, normally symbolizes the person–the personal psychophysical vehicle used to travel through this lifetime.

If, in childhood, someone is traumatized by a tragic auto accident caused by the blinding light of the sun riding low on the horizon of a winter's sunrise, a sunrise may then function for that person as a personal symbol. In this case, a sunrise would symbolize pain and anxiety instead of fresh and inspiring new beginnings. On the other hand, if your birthday is on the thirteenth of the month, the number thirteen may symbolize happiness and abundance (presents) instead of bad luck.

Anything can become a personal symbol. All that is required is that an individual associate it with something peculiar to himself or herself. The meaning is either not inherent to the symbol, or the symbol is not widely encountered.

A good way to try to establish meaning of a personal symbol —or even of a universal symbol that has a particular personal meaning beyond its universal role—is to free-associate about it. To free-associate, simply relax while focusing on the symbol, allowing whatever comes to mind to be openly considered as potentially relevant to the symbol.

In a dream, let us say you unwrap a gift to find it contains packets of M&Ms: peanut candy, which you rarely eat. After you awaken, you let your mind drift back to associations you have about peanut M&Ms: the movies, hiking on the Appalachian Trail, a seventh-grade food fight, sharing them on the ski lift at Snowbird, or when you and Pat watched the sunset on Blackrock Ridge. One of these may strike a chord of recognition or may relate to other aspects of the content of the dream (or coincidence).

We know it is very helpful to take a good look at what is going on in our lives–what is charged with energy–when seeking the meaning of a coincidence or dream. We have seen that this is an excellent source of clues to the meanings of mirror coincidences. Even directional coincidences, although they do not mirror an excited complex, are clearly related to current situations. So a look at what is going on in life can be very helpful for determining the meaning of both personal and universal symbols.

Let us say you have a boss who is very loud and demanding. He insisted that you come up with a proposal in two days, although you knew you needed more time. In your rush to complete the assignment, you did not research the cost parameters thoroughly enough. Subsequently, your boss criticized your proposal because of certain cost factors that had not been adequately dealt with. That night, while rushing in the dark to get some formula for your baby, who is crying with a vengeance, you painfully stub your big toe on the corner of the couch.

If stubbing your toe happened in a dream, we would look back to recent events and current concerns for meaning. The loud and demanding baby might symbolize your loud and demanding boss. Stubbing your toe while rushing in the dark to satisfy the demanding baby would symbolize "stubbing your toe" while rushing "in the dark" at work to satisfy your demanding boss.

But, in this example, you were not dreaming. Therefore, is it a mirror coincidence, in which stubbing your toe reflects harming your status at work while rushing "in the dark" to satisfy your boss? Certainly, it could be. The point for our discussion here, regardless of whether events occur in a coincidence or in a dream, is that the discovery of meaning is greatly aided by looking at current concerns in your life.

THE CONSERVATION OF SYMBOLS

We have seen that a universal symbol may gain a particular meaning that is unique to the individual encountering it, thereby causing it to function as a personal symbol. To go a step further, various different meanings of a symbol may simultaneously be relevant and significant to the circumstances that prompted the emergence of the symbol.

This peculiarity is the expression of a principle termed the conservation of symbols. It is characterized by the precise use of one particular symbol that accurately conveys two or more different, relevant meanings. The different meanings the symbol conveys are all appropriate and may simultaneously represent various levels or different aspects of the psyche. A single symbol or symbolic event may convey meaning relevant to physical needs while simultaneously presenting a different meaning that addresses some practical concern, and perhaps an additional meaning, of a transcendent or spiritual nature.

One example of conservation of symbols occurred with the refrigerator in my mother's coincidence. There, it seems every possible aspect of the refrigerator—function, shape, quality (coldness), size, color—was symbolically appropriate to the coincidence. Yet, in that case, they were all related in various ways to one central meaning.

In the "More Treasure Unearthed" coincidence, which we investigated in chapter two, another example of the conservation of symbols surfaced. In the dream, which was discussed to amplify the symbolic meaning of arrows, the stolen arrows served both as a universal symbol to depict a form of emasculation and a personal symbol to represent my sons being taken from me.

I first encountered the principle of conservation of symbols many years ago, when a friend asked me to interpret a particularly vivid dream. At the time he had the dream, he was an Air Force pilot flying very large eight-engine jet bombers. He was stationed in the upper peninsula of Michigan, which is bordered by the three largest of the Great Lakes: Superior, Michigan, and Huron.

He dreamed that he was a crew member on one of the iron ore ships that ply the lakes. These ships are very long and narrow so they can traverse the locks between the lakes. In his dream, a violent storm was raging, and he was very frightened that his ship would break up in the storm. A number of small, fast, maneuverable boats were speeding around his ship and some other iron ore ships nearby. He wished he were on one of the smaller boats, for he felt they were less likely to rupture from the pounding of the storm.

I knew that my friend had developed considerable anxiety about flying. In fact, at the time of his dream, the Vietnam War was still in progress, and an assignment there was imminent for him, which surely intensified his anxiety. This made interpreting the dream symbols a relatively simple task. Lake Superior, where the ships in the dream were threatened, is so large that land cannot be seen for long periods of time while traversing it. It is like an ocean. The sky, too, is like an ocean, sometimes referred to as the ocean above.

In the dream, the large iron ore ships symbolized the large aircraft that my friend flew in the "ocean above." He was afraid the large, aging bomber would not be able to withstand the forces it might encounter and break apart. The small, fast, maneuverable, sturdy boats symbolized smaller fighter aircraft. Fighter aircraft possess the same characteristics relative to the larger aircraft as the small boats do relative to the long, narrow ships: speed, maneuverability, and the ability to withstand higher G forces. Thus, my friend viewed these as safer, particularly in the hostile environment (symbolized by the stormy weather) in which he anticipated flying.

My friend readily acknowledged that this interpretation struck a chord of recognition in him. In fact, he ultimately had himself taken off flying status, due to what the Air Force classifies as "apprehension of flight."

What took me by surprise was his response to some additional information I provided, simply to give him a different perspective. I did not expect that this new perspective would possess any relevance to the dream, since the first meaning was so clear and verifiable. I simply thought he might be curious to hear a different interpretation of the symbols. I mentioned that Freud would interpret this dream as being symbolic of something anal in nature, about which there was anxiety–that the long narrow ships riding the waves were reminiscent of feces floating in a toilet.

He surprised me by responding that, at that time, he did have a very severe case of hemorrhoids. Then, after a brief pause, he related that he believed he had the dream the night before he had surgery for the hemorrhoids. This certainly revealed the anxiety-provoking nature of the large ships, relative to the small ships, in an entirely different context.

Clearly, the unconscious presented one symbolic situation to represent two entirely different circumstances on different levels of the psyche. Thus, we have here a convincing example of the conservation of symbols.

To add to the amazing versatility of symbols, and the uncanny way they have of relating meaning so precisely, there may be an additional meaning conveyed by my friend's dream. The spontaneous appearance of symbols in dreams and coincidences is certainly not haphazard. One would expect there to be some rationale for symbolically bringing these two situations–the anxiety about flying large bombers and the anxiety about the hemorrhoid operation–together in a dream. The obvious connection is that they are both anxiety-producing circumstances.

However, I now believe the unconscious revealed an even closer connection between these two conditions than just the simultaneous use of the same symbols to represent two different anxiety-provoking circumstances. My explanation is that hemorrhoids are primarily a psychosomatic disorder; their onset is caused by a high level of anxiety. I believe the symbolic connection of my friend's two anxiety-evoking conditions by the unconscious mind was not solely in the interest of conserving symbols, but also hinted at another link that already existed: The severe anxiety about flying precipitated the appearance of the severe case of hemorrhoids, which, in turn, caused more anxiety about the surgery. Thus, it was natural for the unconscious mind to use one symbolic situation to represent two different conditions because they were already connected.

A recent example of conservation of symbols surfaced in a dream Wendy had. She dreamed she was dancing with uninhibited joy and exuberance, naked, at home in front of a large picture window. When she noticed that there were people walking by on the sidewalk in front of the house, looking at her, she realized she did not even care. This is a very positive dream.

In coincidences and dreams, one's home possesses symbolic meaning similar to that of a personal vehicle. Just as a personal vehicle symbolizes the psychophysical self in which one journeys through this lifetime, one's home invariably symbolizes the body and personality within which one resides—that same psychophysical self. This house-as-person symbol is one of the most common symbols in dreams.

Many people wear masks; they project a public personality that is different (perhaps considerably so) from their true nature. Jung called this the persona. The fact that Wendy was joyfully dancing naked, and was not disturbed by being viewed in that state, symbolizes a healthy self-acceptance and confidence in her own unadorned self. It says she is comfortable with allowing herself to be viewed as she really is, without the layers of protective psychological garments that many people wear to conceal their true self from others. The large picture window in the dream reinforces this interpretation, as a picture window makes it easy to see inside a house. In other words, the unadorned true self is clearly presented, not disguised or obscured.

However, this same dream sequence conveyed another, more direct meaning. In this age, the media, and particularly the abundance of women's magazines, ubiquitously promote the necessity of possessing and maintaining some mythical, ideal body and appearance. This can result in real insecurities in even very attractive women, not to mention those who vary from the "ideal" appearance. Real-life circumstances indicated that both the first, more symbolic interpretation was correct, as well as a second interpretation in which meaning was more directly conveyed.

In addition to expressing the feeling that it was no longer necessary to conceal her natural, spontaneous, essential self beneath protective coverings, the dream reflected the more straightforward meaning of an abandonment of insecurities about her physical appearance for a healthy acceptance. Here again, the unconscious used one symbol to convey meaning on two different levels.

ACTING UPON ANALYSIS

By now, we should be familiar with the basic steps to determining symbolic meaning. The first is to identify the essential quality and function of the symbol in regard to the primary ways it is experienced or viewed. Next, we need to attend to the particular context in which the symbol appears in the coincidence (or dream) in order to determine the specific meaning being conveyed. Finally, we need to appraise the psychological and psychophysical circumstances surrounding the emergence of the symbolic event— the coincidence—paying particular attention to those situations or complexes that are invested with psychic energy by the protagonist. This final step helps to deduce the meaning of a symbol if we have not already been able to determine it and helps to substantiate or refute meaning that has been tentatively resolved.

An additional tool that can be helpful is the method of free association. And, finally, it is important to maintain a totally open, even creative, mind when regarding the possible significance of a symbol. For example, a lone white shoe in a dream or coincidence could very easily symbolize something associated with a dinner party ten years ago, in which one white shoe was temporarily lost.

A few additional considerations for the practical evaluation of symbols include the following: treat all the details and accessories accompanying a coincidence as having potential significance. Even a stranger or mere casual acquaintance who becomes involved in a coincidence is likely to be a participant for a reason, not merely an accidental member of the cast. The person may personify some aspect of yourself or be symbolic of some other situation.

The place a coincidence occurs, just as the setting in a dream, should be viewed as tentatively meaningful and perhaps symbolic. It is best to evaluate all the details of a coincidence or dream as being potentially subjective—as being related to the subject, which is you.

When acting on the meaning you have concluded a coincidence possesses, do so cautiously. If associated circumstances do not substantiate your interpretation of symbolic meaning, it is not advisable to change the course of action you would have pursued had the coincidence not occurred. Even an opinion of someone or something should not be altered based solely upon your interpretation of symbolic events. At most, you should consider a newly revealed potential course of action as a possible option—an avenue that has been opened for further consideration. Ask yourself whether it would be among the logical alternatives if the coincidence had not occurred. Consult someone whose judgment you trust. Even when other circumstances point in the same direction, proceed cautiously. A frequent reappraisal of the appropriateness of your actions should be performed. Your reappraisals must be able to reinforce the course of action taken.

We now have the necessary ingredients to extract meaning from the symbols encountered in our dream and daytime worlds. The only additional ingredients needed for familiarity with the role of symbols and confidence in your ability to discover meaning are attention to their presence and practice in analyzing them.

At first, some symbols will remain a complete puzzle. This is particularly true of dream symbols. Our unconscious minds have an immense amount of data at their disposal; and, in dreams, they sometimes use this material in very mysterious ways. However, our dreams are fertile ground for developing our symbol analysis skills. In investigating dreams, you also will learn more about yourself and how you relate to your environment.

The symbols encountered in the waking state—in coincidences—seem to me to be generally easier to analyze, particularly those in directional coincidences, which, after all, are there to guide us. So, we should expect their meaning to be discernible. Whenever we encounter a coincidence or tentative coincidence, even minor ones, we should take the attitude that, just for our own entertainment, and possibly for our benefit, we're going to see if we can discern meaning—a minor mystery to be unraveled.

A FEATHER IN THE BREEZE REVISITED

We began this chapter by looking at the meaning of the white feather floating about at the beginning and end of the movie *Forrest Gump*. The floating feather served as a metaphor for Forrest and his method of responding to the forces buffeting his life. I noted then that the feather symbolized a bit more than that most immediate meaning. Now that we have investigated the rules of symbol analysis, let us look a little further into the meaning of that symbol.

I cannot say for sure what Eric Roth (who adapted Winston Groom's book for the screenplay) had in mind with the floating feather. But, in truth, his exact intent with the feather imagery is not critical to its symbolic meaning. Our unconscious minds sometimes use images in a symbolic way that we may not even be consciously aware of, and not just in our dreams. I was surprised many years ago to discover that a children's book I had written turned out to be very symbolic. Yet I did not recognize its symbolic content until after it was completed. In any case, I am relatively confident that the meaning discussed at the beginning of this chapter, and that which we will look at here, is consistent with the intention of the symbol's creator.

Two qualities that are immediately apparent about the feather are that it is white and that it is unconfined. The feather was not attached to something, like a chicken or hawk or headdress. And it could have been most any color: black, red, or gray. But it was pure white and floating free.

After the feather came to rest on his foot, Forrest picked it up and placed it in a book. The book was *Curious George*, a children's book about a monkey. Again, the feather did not have to land on Forrest's foot, and Forrest did not have to pick it up. Once he did, though, he did not have to put it in the book, and the book could have been about anything. It did not have to be about a monkey. With symbol analysis—whether we are analyzing a coincidence, dream, or events in a movie—the details are treated as being meaningful. We know white is associated with purity and sometimes with heaven. The air above, where the feather was when we first saw it, is also associated with heaven. It is logical to conclude that the feather symbolizes the soul—Forrest's soul in particular (it came to rest on his foot) and humankind's soul in general. When the feather is floating in the air at the beginning and end of the movie, it symbolizes the soul when it is free, in heaven, and not confined to a physical body.

Curious George, the monkey who received the feather (soul), symbolizes Forrest in particular, although again, by extension, it represents the rest of humankind, of which Forrest is an example. A monkey, as humankind's closest relative—and a lower relative—emphasizes the human physical or lower self (in contrast to the soul). Also, in being less intelligent than a human, it points to Forrest, who was said to be of borderline intelligence. In fact, the monkey imagery implies that humankind in general is frequently more primitive or of a lower order when inhabiting a body, which many of the negative situations in the movie bear out: war, segregation, Jenny's treatment as a child, assassinations.

The feather, when placed in the book *Curious George*, symbolizes the soul when in a physical body: one's life, Forrest's life. A book can symbolize a lifetime. The pages that are turned are the days or years of the lifetime—the passing events. The beginning and end of the book are the beginning and end of physical existence.

At the end of the movie, Forrest opens *Curious George*, and the feather floats free again. The soul returns to the heavens above, at least for a while. The implication is that of an ongoing process—the feather coming and going. In the movie, death is accepted without fear. Most of the people Forrest loved die in the movie: Momma, Jenny, and Bubba. And Lt. Dan was angry because Forrest didn't allow him to die. Death is accepted as part of the process—the feather's coming and going again. "It's just my time" is Momma's simple response of acceptance when asked by Forrest why she is dying. Of course, Forrest does not die in the end; the feather (soul) floating free at the end is more an implication that the cycle of life and death will continue.

The symbol of the white feather is also is a perfect example of the principle of the conservation of symbols. Both the symbolic meaning of the feather presented at the beginning of this chapter and the one presented here are very valid, powerful, and pertinent to the theme conveyed by the movie. The meanings are quite distinct, although somewhat related. The correctness and effectiveness of remaining true to oneself, no matter what forces buffet one's journey through life, and the transient, ongoing process of life and death are both poetically conveyed by the use of this one symbol. Congratulations are in order for Eric Roth not only for his genius in coming up with such an appropriate symbol, but also for his capacity to be in touch with the creative, unconscious self from which such a true and pure example of the conservation of symbols must have arisen.

THE WORLD AS SYMBOL

There is one more aspect of symbols that should be touched upon in any serious investigation of their significance. However, it is somewhat technical and a little difficult to appreciate fully. It is also not really vital to the comprehension of coincidences, nor to the analysis of the symbols that are employed in them. So if the material in the next few pages seems a little too far removed from the practical concerns of daily life, it may be neglected without hampering our investigation of the meaning and use of coincidence.

Yet, because it is important to provide a thorough treatment of the subject, mention should be made of how symbols are viewed by some intellectuals, philosophers, metaphysicians, scientists, and artists relative to the overall scheme of the world. Furthermore, this perception of the role of symbols does have relevance to later discussions on the metaphysical foundation of coincidence.

The most representative and prevalent of various related perspectives, which view all of creation as symbolic, is found in the theory of correspondences. In a well-researched work entitled *A Dictionary of Symbols*, J. E. Cirlot gives correspondence theory prominence in accounting for the full role of symbols in all creation. His perspective is one maintained by a significant number of intellectual explorers in both the West and East. Cirlot's observations include the following:

> The theory of "correspondences" is basic to symbolist tradition. The implications and scope of this theory are beyond measure, and any valid study into the ultimate nature of the universe must take it into account. . . . It is founded upon the assumption that all cosmic phenomenon are limited and serial and that they appear as scales or series on separate planes; but this condition is neither chaotic nor neutral, for the components of one series are linked with those of another in their essence and in their ultimate significance. (Cirlot 1962, 60)

That statement could use a little clarification, which will be provided. However, it does not lack conviction, for the assertion that "any valid study into the ultimate nature of the universe must take it into account" certainly illustrates the important role Cirlot and many others assign to correspondence theory. Emanuel Swedenborg, one who was convinced of its role in creation, may be able to provide clarity.

Swedenborg was a most remarkable individual. Fluent in nine languages, he published well over 400 works on a great variety of subjects, the vast majority of which concerned spiritual matters. Swedenborg backed up his convictions concerning that which transcends the material world by his own often-demonstrated capacity to transcend the boundaries of the physical realm himself. Some of his well-documented feats of that nature will be presented in chapter four. To Swedenborg, the "science of correspondences" was not mere theory, but absolute fact. A good picture of Swedenborg's conception of correspondences is presented by George Trobridge in *Swedenborg: Life and Teachings*:

> The concept of correspondences is based on the fact that everything outward and visible has an inward and

spiritual cause. . . . The whole universe is, indeed "the time-vesture of the Eternal," and symbolic in every detail. "All visible things are emblems," because they are created in correspondence with Divine ideas. The "Science of Correspondences" is the science that enables us to understand their inner reality. . . . As outward nature is the embodiment of Divine ideas, and man was created "in the image and likeness of God," there is a correspondence of all things in man with all things of the physical universe. . . . All things in general and in particular which exist in the created universe have such a correspondence with all things in man in general and in particular, that it may be said that man also is a kind of universe. . . . The correspondence of outward nature with the human mind and life, is only a limited example of this great law, which extends throughout the universe, by various degrees to the material plane in every world, and every plane of life is related to all others by correspondence. (Trobridge 1976, 150-154)

This view is not one held by those on the fringe of reality. It might better be characterized as that which is held by those who have approached the heart of reality. Carl Jung, for one, was indebted to Swedenborg's insight and supported his perspective. Jung said, "In some way or another we are part of a single, all embracing psyche, a single 'greatest man,' the homo maximus, to quote Swedenborg" (Jung 1959, 86). Jung said his principle of synchronicity was a differentiation of the "concept of correspondence, sympathy, and harmony. It is based not on philosophical assumptions but on empirical experience and experimentation" (Jung 1973, 115). Jung further elaborates:

The animate world is the larger circle, man is the "Limbus Minor," the smaller circle. He is the microcosm. Consequently, everything without is within, everything above is below. Between all things in the larger and smaller circles reigns "correspondence," a notion that culminates in

Swedenborg's homo maximus as a gigantic anthropo-
morphization of the universe. (Jung 1966, 9)

Swedenborg viewed the universe as "symbolic in every detail"
and, like Plato, perceived all visible things as representations of
divine ideas. All things of the physical plane of existence correspond
to—are representations of—underlying generative archetypes, or
patterns, in the realms preceding physical manifestation—the
supraconscious or spiritual realms. From a unitary generative
source, ideas—or archetypes—descend from one plane to the next,
accruing particularity, to coalesce on the material plane of creation. That is one aspect of correspondence.

A second aspect is that since all of "nature is the embodiment of
Divine ideas, and man was created 'in the image and likeness of
God,'" it follows that all aspects of nature are reflections, emblems,
and symbols of corresponding characteristics of man. This is the
perspective that everything without is within, that humans are the
microcosm that embraces the macrocosm within themselves.
Thus, a certain mood, emotion, or human quality corresponds
with and is symbolized by a particular musical note, a specific
color, a type of tree, a certain animal, a particular mineral or element, a flower or plant, a planet or constellation, and so on—all
symbolic of each other and all representations of underlying qualities that are found in humans.

This brings to mind the findings of research on the near-death
experience, which is encountered by those who, for a short period
of time, have been clinically dead, but then revived. In the out-of-
body state these people experience, many report encountering
deceased individuals whose human traits are now perceived as patterns of light and sound. This is not unlike the perceptions of those
who can view human auras. They see specific patterns of color,
shape, and intensity in the aura surrounding each individual,
which may change according to the individual's health and psychological state.

This perception of reality—the mystical apprehension of reality
that science is now awakening to—if it embodies universal truths,
should transcend cultures and ages. The true visionaries of all cul-

tures in all times should have tapped the same wellspring of reality. This, in fact, is the case. We find Meister Eckhart saying essentially the same thing in the fourteenth century as Swedenborg said in the eighteenth, and Jung reiterated in the twentieth:

> I cannot see anything unless it bears some likeness to myself, nor can I know anything unless it is analogous to me. God has hidden all things in himself. They are not this and that, individually distinct, but rather, they are one with unity. . . "The shell must be cracked apart if what is in it is to come out; for if you want the kernel, you must break the shell." And therefore, if you want to discover nature's nakedness, you must destroy its symbols and the farther you get in, the nearer you come to its essence. (Blakney 1941, 148)

When Eckhart says we must destroy nature's symbols, it is, of course, not meant literally, but symbolically. Besides saying that to see and know things they must have some likeness to ourselves, he is saying we must penetrate the barrier that the shells of superficial knowledge present to knowing the essence within. Vivekananda, the Hindu of the East, perceived the same thing in the nineteenth century: "In one sense we cannot think but in symbols; words themselves are symbols of thought. In another sense everything in the universe may be looked upon as a symbol. The whole universe is a symbol, and God is the essence behind" (Vivekananda 1989, 72).

Much more could be said regarding the symbolic significance and interconnectedness of all phenomena and its relevance in reflecting the qualities of humankind. However, I do not want to belabor this esoteric vein of thought here. It has been briefly offered at the conclusion of this investigation of symbols primarily to illustrate that the role of symbols in our lives may be far more extensive than we are normally aware of.

4 Coincidence and the Quality of Life

IN EARLIER CHAPTERS, we have seen how directional coincidences can assist us both in the specific situations that challenge us and in enhancing the overall tone of our life. The more aware we become of directional coincidences in our lives, the more we will be able to use them for greater purpose. Paying attention to these vital forces allows us to make choices that will increase the overall contentment and quality of our lives.

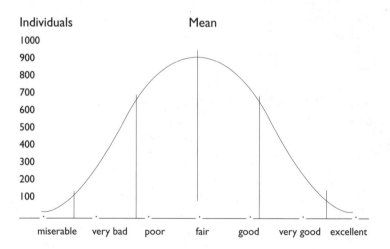

The bell curve on the previous page depicts the normal pattern of views held by a population of individuals about their quality of life. When we think about how satisfied we are with our quality of life, we are essentially evaluating how happy we are, or rather, how content. There are differences between happiness and contentment; different images probably come to mind when you envision being as happy as you could possibly be, versus being totally content.

In the first part of this chapter, we will compare those two subjective measures of well-being: happiness and contentment. The bell curve will be used to help illustrate how it is important not to be satisfied with an average degree of contentment—the level shared by the masses. The way that directional coincidences can help enhance our position on the "bell curve of contentment" will also be illustrated.

In the second part of this chapter, we will look at a few remarkable individuals who have transcended the normal boundaries of human knowledge and behavior. They represent the complete realization of a different type of variable. These individuals, who have achieved the full degree of the potential for development we all possess, are among the tiny fraction of a percent at the extreme right of a bell curve that depicts the degrees to which humans actualize human potential. Since throughout history (including the present) there have consistently been a few individuals who have fully developed their resources to transcend the boundaries that limit the rest of us, it would seem to be a capability we all possess.

These individuals, and some of their accomplishments, are presented because of the comprehension of reality they share. In order for them to have transcended the illusory boundaries that normally confine humankind, it is clear they must have a good understanding of the realities behind the appearances in this world. In the final chapter, the wisdom that is the product of the exclusive segment of humanity those presented represent will be emphasized to help explain how our physical world can spontaneously align itself to provide the coincidences investigated here. Examples of the feats of those presented in this chapter are provided to help validate the perception of reality shared by those at the far right of the bell curve of human potential achieved, and to inspire the rest of us to use the guidance regularly offered by directional coincidences to lead us closer to the contentment and freedom they enjoy.

THE BELL CURVE

Anyone who has ever taken a course in statistics is familiar with the bell curve. The bell curve is the curve on a graph that depicts the normal variability of some characteristic or aptitude tabulated in a population, geographic area, period of history, and so on. The characteristic tabulated could be anything from degree of satisfaction in romance among New York City residents to the normal July rainfall in Bombay over the last century. The bell curve on the first page of this chapter depicts a probable sampling of feelings of well-being in the average population. The number of cases that fall within various degrees of satisfaction is on the vertical axis. Most cases will be grouped near the average, or mean, of whatever is being measured. Thus, the curve is highest there, at the dome of the bell. In this case, the mean assessment of well-being is "fair." The actual scores, traits, or measurements are depicted on the horizontal axis of the bell curve, with fewer cases the further they diverge to either side of the mean. Thus, the curve tapers off symmetrically on either side to form the silhouette of a bell.

There is one very useful feature of bell curves that I would like to touch upon before looking at the differences between contentment and happiness. It is called the standard deviation, and it is represented on bell curve charts by the Greek letter sigma (σ). We usually need to identify more than the mean (average) of a population in assessing some characteristic; it is useful to know whether scores or measurements are clustered very tightly about the mean, or whether there is a wide range of variability in measurements.

The standard deviation is the average amount by which scores or traits differ from the score that is the mean of all the scores, or measurements.[1] In the normal distributions that bell curves depict,

---

1. By definition, the standard deviation is actually a little more technical. It is the square root of the mean of the squares of the amount by which each case departs from the mean of all cases.

over two-thirds of any sample population (68%) will always fall within one standard deviation from the mean. In other words, only one-third of the population will differ from the mean by more than the average amount that all scores vary from it. So the standard deviation readily identifies that which may be considered the *average segment* of a population as well as how much variability there is in that average group. It also provides the not-very-startling conclusion that in most cases, the great majority of the population is grouped among the average.

THE GOAL OF HAPPINESS
VS. THE PROCESS OF CONTENTMENT

Most human variables conform to bell curve distributions. For some variables, we are quite content to be among the masses— that is, to be within the two-thirds of the population who are within one standard deviation from the mean. In other cases, we might prefer to be outside of the norm. We might prefer to be a little thinner, better looking, wittier, wealthier, less anxious, or taller than those in the dome of the bell.

Some variables are impossible to change, while others may be modified without much difficulty. If you think your feet are too big, the only thing you can change is your attitude. And if you are not happy with your height, well, the rack went out of style a long time ago. But there are many ways we can improve our health, ways to increase strength and stamina, and vary our weight—again and again.

Physical variables are easy to define and measure. Psychological variables, such as attitudes, emotions, feelings, and even intelligence, are less precise. That ambiguity is characteristic of the variable that is the primary focus here. How many of us can articulate, right now, the most important goal in life—that which is the single best measure of satisfaction and fulfillment? The identification of such a variable—valid and appropriate for us all—is the necessary first step to establish the means of attaining it.

Happiness is one such quality that readily comes to mind. Even for those who object, stating that, for them, there is a more important goal—such as reducing crime and violence, saving the whale, curbing the worldwide population explosion, or having a whole lot of money—happiness encompasses attainment of the particular goals that are individually important.

Yet there may be a couple of difficulties with singling out happiness as the most important enduring quality to be achieved in life. In the first place, one would expect that, as an enduring state, the highest degree of the most desirable quality is what we would all hope to enjoy. When we hear people verbalize the higher states of happiness—"I'm soooo happy"; "This is the happiest day of my life"—we associate it with peak experiences: parties, celebrations, the winning of an award or contest or the lottery. It implies a state of intense excitement, something that, in reality, may be fun now and then, but that most of us can only experience for so long before we have had enough. Ecstasy is probably the highest state of happiness. And all-out, tingling ecstasy may be great, but a person cannot really function when he or she is ecstatic. All someone can really do in such a state is to be ecstatic, kind of like being a bright neon light. But most of us want to do more than just glow in the dark.

Recently, I looked up *happiness* in the local library. I found well over a hundred books listed that dealt with the subject of happiness. Most dealt with surefire ways to obtain happiness. In general, these books might loosely be categorized as the offspring of Norman Vincent Peale, who some decades ago wrote *The Power of Positive Thinking*, a book that became immensely popular. For the most part, these books are variations on a theme he recommended, which is to think positively about the attainment of your particular desires and they will be achieved.

One variation of this technique is the positive visualization that many athletes use, with which they visualize themselves perfectly performing the event in which they are to compete. The idea is not to program the muscles to function in a specific way, nor is it to increase the flow of adrenaline by getting "psyched up." It is to create consciously, in one's own mind, the situation one desires to have materialized and an aura of positive anticipation of success. The expectation is that reality will then mirror that which one had consciously created in one's mind. This same technique is recommended to enhance the prospect of success by those who are to make a presentation, for instance, in a business or academic setting.

The idea that the mind is a powerful tool for change is almost ridiculously self-evident. We need only look around the room or turn on the television or the computer to witness the products of the mind. Of course, the concept these books promote goes beyond the ordinary functioning of the mind, with the idea that positive thoughts spontaneously blossom into situations that reflect them. This is more startling, but our examination of mirror coincidences has provided proof that, at least some of the time, this does happen.

However, the investigation of mirror coincidences also revealed some of the problems with relying on intense mental energy to shape our psychophysical world. First of all, results are far from assured, and the period of time in which energy must be invested is uncertain, so the source of energy may become drained before success materializes. Second, we do not always know what will provide us with happiness, much less what is best for us, even though we are constantly informed by the media that these include a new car, new clothes, a new look, a better brand of beer: things obtained with money, power, and position. That is happiness. And what else? You have got to be involved in a relationship—even if it is not the right one—to be cool and happy.

This search for happiness may just be a gigantic escape mechanism. Maybe we are afraid to look at life, at the big picture, to see how we fit into the overall scheme of things, so we escape by being consumed with the *pursuit* of happiness and with the things we are told will provide it. The irony is that, if we could see the big picture and our relationship to it, we would realize there is no cause for alarm. Happiness need not be pursued. Once we dismantle the fortress we have erected to protect ourselves, we find that contentment and bliss are our very nature.

Contentment may be a much more appropriate enduring goal. Contentment is the state in which one feels satisfied and fulfilled. It is being gratified and pleased with one's existence.

The cultivation of contentment is a different type of activity from the pursuit of happiness. It is like taking a walk in the country in contrast to a rush through the department store of life during its annual "Pursuit of Happiness" supersale. Contentment is more *process*-oriented while happiness is more *goal*-oriented. Consequently, in paying attention to the process, we are allowed to relate with interest to what is going on around us: the way the dishes are being washed, the garden is being hoed, the client is being coaxed; to the moon's playing hide-and-seek behind the clouds, to the tail lights' reflection on the wet road ahead, the puppy digging in the tulip bed.

As David Bohm observed earlier, flux, change, the process is the constant reality in our world. Things come and go. The process remains. When we focus on the process, we are allowed to focus on excellence for its own sake and the substance of the present instead of the shadow of the future and the things it may produce. A wise friend once said, "The reason the moment we are in right now is called the present is because it is a gift." The cultivation of contentment allows us to appreciate that gift.

As with happiness, contentment is not in conflict with possessing specific objectives, for that is encompassed by contentment. The housewife and mother's greatest desire may be simply to be the best wife and mother she can be, just as the pediatrician's highest goal may be to provide the best health care she can. Contentment would then, to a large degree, simply be a function of how well these qualities were realized.

Yet unlike being unbelievably happy—being ecstatic—being totally content does not imply an excessive or inordinate measure of something. In response to the question of what would make someone happiest, you might hear the reply "to be fabulously wealthy." But it is quite unlikely you would receive that reply in response to the question of what would make one totally content. It just does not fit. In fact, one definition of content is "having the desires limited to whatever one has." Someone who has achieved this has attained a great degree of freedom, without limiting aspirations.

There is a curious similarity between contentment and lack of boredom. Some people are never bored. Placed in an empty room, they still would not be bored. They would easily find something with which to amuse themselves, for the manifold mysteries of life fill them, leaving no room for boredom. Similarly, there are a few who have realized total contentment. No matter what circumstances they experience, they are content. This does not mean that they have accomplished everything they wish to or intend to. It means they are able to enjoy the journey as well as the safe arrival at their destination. It might also mean that they possess a particular ability to perceive perfection where others do not.

Suppose a large group of people was asked to respond anonymously to a question that expresses more or less the following: "How content are you with your life—your existence right now and your anticipation of the future, the future both near and far, including your concept of that which lies beyond?" What would be the average level of contentment?

A recently published quality of life survey noted that the majority of respondents identified their level of happiness as "fairly happy." So it is reasonable to assume that "somewhat content" would be the predominant level of contentment in a normal population. The group's contentment bell curve, with seven levels of contentment to choose from, would look similar to the one below:

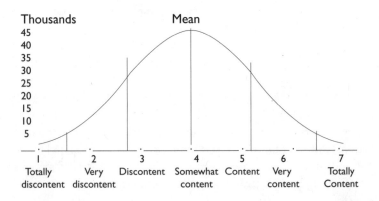

There are some important points that may be made in regard to the contentment bell curve: (1) The great mass of humanity is less than very content, and probably not even "content." (2) There are practical actions we can take to improve our sense of contentment. (3) It is important both for us individually, and for the society we live in, to progress toward the right of the curve—toward greater contentment. (4) Therefore, if you or I am in that average realm, or even more content than that, we should not resign ourselves to remaining there. (5) Becoming more content may merely require a change of perspective, although more substantial changes may also need to be accomplished. (6) In either case, attending to the directional coincidences in our lives can be a very effective means of moving toward total contentment.

It is important for us, individually and culturally, to progress toward the right of the curve. The importance for the individual is evident. When we are content, we are healthier psychologically and physically (since most physical maladies are at least in part psychosomatic). When we are content, we are satisfied, at peace, and feel a harmonious connectedness with the world about us. And when we are discontent, we covet, which has significant negative consequences.

Think of all the difficulties caused for an individual, and those around him or her, when that person covets the spouse, house, wealth, or profession of others. When we are content, we are able to connect with others as equals because we are at ease with, and feel satisfied with, our own circumstances. Thus, when other people's circumstances vary from our own, it does not lessen our natural tendency to relate to them in a positive way, without artifice, inhibition, or ulterior motives.

One who is not content, covets, which is the cause of much crime and discomfort in this culture. Whether we consider a corporate takeover artist committing white-collar crime or a criminal on the street, the covetousness that accompanies a lack of contentment is likely the primary cause of the crime and many other interpersonal difficulties, as well. So when we foster a sense of contentment, it extends beyond our personal sense of well-being to provide practical consequences for us, for those with whom we interact, and for our culture.

Nurturing contentment may appear to be just another utopian formula, but it is really quite practical and not difficult to achieve on the individual level, where all large-scale change commences. After all, an increase in contentment may only require a different perspective, a change of attitude. That is one of the ways in which the quest for contentment differs from the pursuit of happiness.

How do we go about cultivating contentment? A good first step is to begin to melt the thing called ego, the thing that separates us from, and pits us against, our own humanity. The ego makes us small, isolates us, blinds us, and deafens us to the symphony in which we play. The ego screams that it knows what is best for us, but its track record does not encourage scrutiny.

But if we cannot count on the ego for guidance, where will we find it? The point is we do not need to find it. It is right here, all about us. All we have to do is open ourselves up to the process—to the knowledge provided by this incredible chameleon classroom we live in. An old Sanskrit verse conveys a truth about God's creation we seldom perceive:

That is perfect. This is perfect.
From the perfect comes the perfect.
If you take the perfect from the perfect
The perfect remains. (Siva Mahimna Stotram)

We need to become conscious of the mysterious process we are already part of, which is participating in the play of perfection. One way we can open our awareness to perfection is to investigate the possibility of being provided with guidance by directional coincidences.

When we are sensitive to the guidance provided by directional coincidences, we still do the things we like to do, engage in the activities we find rewarding, and continue with our careers. However, while doing this, at least for a while, we do not need to be excessively concerned with whether we are using our time most efficiently, whether we are precisely investing our resources in the most correct way to attain the goals we seek, and whether those goals are appropriate. We can take a break. At least temporarily, we can turn those responsibilities over to the divine source of wisdom.

We can simply conduct a study to see if the appropriateness of our activities will be revealed to us by directional coincidences. For a while, we may allow ourselves the luxury of just being content with observing what is happening around us, simply enjoying the processes in which we are participating, while casually investigating whether there are ways we can contribute to the greater harmony and beauty of the flow of events. We can relax, and calmly, with a sense of curiosity, see if personal guidance will be provided.

Before long, guidance to change course where needed will be received, as will confirmations to hold steady when that is correct. One at the helm of a sailboat does not simply point the bow toward some distant destination. He or she must be sensitive to what is going on around him or her if he or she is to employ the breezes and changing currents to be propelled to the destination. Similarly, if prevailing currents and forces for change provided by directional coincidences are responded to in each of our voyages through life, success is assured.

Receptivity to directional coincidences fosters contentment in a number of ways. First, the burden of deciding what to do with our lives—whether according to others' expectations or our own speculations—is lessened. We have opened the lines of communication to the divine source of knowledge, which knows the particular things that will provide each of us with fulfillment and contentment much better than we do.

Second, in consequence, we are able to focus on the process at play from moment to moment instead of being consumed by concerns about attainment of various goals of uncertain intrinsic value. This allows us to participate more completely and beautifully with everybody and everything in our environment, so that we come to have a greater sense of our larger self, as a self without boundary.

Third, as the wisdom of directional coincidences is increasingly revealed by the tangible results of responding to the guidance provided, and as our sense of oneness and harmony with all of creation grows, our confidence in the "big picture" and the perfection of our place in it is nurtured. Thus, our contentment is not just in the rewards of the moment, but of what lies in the future, including the lifetimes that are to follow.

Consequently, if for a time we experience difficulties and disappointments, we can still retain our sense of contentment. For we have come to see that they are just a part of the process, part of the changing landscape of our journey toward a grander perfection. Every point in the process—whether it is difficult or a breeze—affords the same opportunity of responding constructively and positively, increasing contentment in our interplay with the dynamic field of force and phenomena that are part of our larger self.

The posture encouraged here is not new. It is the common perspective of the mystic, who perceives his or her own harmony and oneness with all of creation and with the Source from which creation flows. One such individual was Emanuel Swedenborg, whose accomplishments we will examine in the beginning of the next section. The fact that the foremost Zen Buddhist scholar of this century, D. T. Suzuki, wrote a book about him (*Swedenborg: Buddha of the North*) underscores the high esteem in which Swedenborg is held by scholars of both the West and East.

In that book, Suzuki quotes the New Testament to support Swedenborg's emphasis on the importance of innocence: "Let the children come to me; do not try to stop them; for the kingdom of heaven belongs to such as these. I tell you, whoever does not accept the kingdom of God like a child will never enter it" (Mark 10:14, Luke 18:16). Swedenborg says: "Those who are in a state of innocence attribute nothing of good to themselves, but regard all things as received and ascribe them to the Lord . . . and wish to be led by Him and not by themselves." Suzuki adds, "As for the source of innocence, it spontaneously floods the inner life when we completely give up our own thoughts" (Suzuki 1996, 78).

Perhaps some might still suspect that this encouragement of innocence—of giving up one's own thoughts to accept divine guidance while recognizing God's role in whatever good we may be the instrument of—is simply for gaining admission to heaven when that time comes. Meister Eckhart sets the record straight on the practical power of this posture in the present:

> This is a sure and necessary truth, that he who gives up to God his own will, captures God and binds him, so that God can do nothing but what that person wills! Give your will over completely to God and he will give you his in return, so fully and without reserve, that the will of God shall be your own human will ... but he cannot belong to anyone who has not first become his. (Blakney 1941, 175)

The power and clarity of Eckhart's exhortation leaves no doubt of the practical consequences, here on earth, of aligning ourselves with what God presents to us as his will for us. It even extends beyond the mere achievement of success, with the access to resources far beyond our own, in that "the will of God shall be your own human will."

God's guidance is certainly not limited to the dramatic directional coincidences with which we are occasionally presented. All that we encounter, whether appearing to have a rational cause or not, is, in essence, the directional coincidences provided by God for our guidance. Eckhart says:

> You should know that to those persons who put themselves completely in God's hands, and seek with all diligence to do his will, all that God gives is best of all. . . . Even if something there is that seems better to you, it should not; for, since God wills it this way and not otherwise, it must necessarily be best for you. . . . Now likely, you will ask: "How shall I know whether it is the will of God or not?" As for that, know that if it were not God's will it could not be. (Blakney 1941, 183)

At this point, I would like to introduce a cute, little, green creature called an inchworm. The skinny inchworm is about an inch long, maybe a bit more. However, it is not its length that gives the inchworm its name. The name stems from its means of locomotion. The inchworm generally keeps the middle of its body elevated to form a hump above the ground. When it travels, it does so by repeatedly moving first the front portion of its body forward, and then the rear portion. This is accomplished by lifting the front part slightly while lowering and extending the raised and curved middle portion, causing the forward extension of the head and front part. This movement is followed by the drawing forward of the rear portion, causing the middle portion to again be elevated above the surface in a hump. Once again, this is succeeded by the extension of the front part. Thus, the inchworm "inches" forward an inch at a time.

The reason that I introduce the inchworm is that its shape and manner of locomotion incorporate the central points of this chapter. Not only is its silhouette that of a bell curve, but its manner of moving steadily forward, inch by inch, is how one progresses to the right of the bell curve of contentment.

The journey, the mission offered to each of us in regard to contentment, is to move gradually and steadily from the amorphous mass of mediocrity in the middle of the bell curve toward the rarefied realm of total contentment. One key to success is receptivity to the guidance personally tailored to each of our journeys, provided by the Supraconsciousness inherent in all of creation.

When we are responsive to the wisdom contained in the seemingly fortuitous circumstances of directional coincidences, we come to see they are signposts for the wise, showing the way to richness and transcendence. Thus, our contentment increases as we become more confident of the correctness of the process in which we are engaged, that of steadily moving toward greater awareness and fulfillment. And as we do, the rest of the cultural organism we are part of does also, so that the bell curve of humanity slowly moves toward that secret destination where the individual suddenly finds that the inchworm became a caterpillar along the way and now is about to unfold its wings.

HUMANS WHO HAVE
REALIZED HUMAN POTENTIAL

Twentieth-century scientists discovered that time and space are relative and illusory, that the solidity of material objects is also an illusion, for they are not solid at all, but simply enduring, dynamic patterns of energy. However, they are not able to demonstrate in their personal behavior the truth of their new-found knowledge. They cannot, for instance, see tomorrow today, pass a ball through a wall, or instantly transport themselves to some distant destination. They have not transcended the illusory nature of our material world.

Many, no doubt, consider the idea of personally transcending the limitations of time and space to be pure fantasy, that the bell curve delineating the limits of knowledge attainable by human beings does not extend that far. The ability to transcend the apparent barriers of our material world is not considered by most to be within humankind's reach. Yet this is not true.

On the extreme right of a bell curve depicting the degree to which humans actualize human potential, there actually are individuals, and have been individuals throughout history, who *know* that space, time, and the physical world are illusory. Historically, there has been a very slight percentage (a small percentage of one percent) of human beings who have attained the knowledge necessary to demonstrate that, for them, the boundaries of our physical world are insubstantial.

In a number of books of the last two to three decades, recent revolutionary findings of physics have been repeatedly compared with similar long-held perspectives of Eastern metaphysics. Western scientists no longer scoff at the mystic's comprehension of reality, for they have found the perceptions of the mystic, particularly the sophisticated metaphysics of the East, to be correct.

Yet the first reason the metaphysics of the mystic should be accorded respect is even more compelling. Each individual is a kind of universe, a microcosm in which the essence of the things and activities of all of creation may be found. As such, he or she should have the capacity to actualize, to personify, the true nature of reality. If the mystic's knowledge is real, is realized and not just rhetoric, he or she should be able to transcend the illusory boundaries of the insubstantial material world. Saints, sages, and Siddhas of India—and from elsewhere as well—have throughout history achieved just that. The following examples of abilities possessed by those who reside at the far right of "the bell curve of human potential achieved" are given to help substantiate their comprehension of reality. For realizations attained by individuals such as these will play an important role in establishing the metaphysical basis of coincidence in the next chapter.

The East is not the exclusive province of the mystic. There have always been mystics in the West as well. The religious affiliation of a mystic is of little importance; a mystic is first and foremost a mystic, regardless of religious affiliation. There have been and are Christian mystics, Jewish mystics, Muslim mystics, Hindu mystics, Taoist mystics, Buddhist mystics, and Native American mystics. For the mystic, many paths lead to God; one's religious affiliation is like one's apparel for the journey: a matter of personal preference.

Nevertheless, the most fruitful mystical traditions are in the East. This is because mysticism has been cultivated there, has been the staple of the garden there for a very long time. In the East, mysticism has had the opportunity to be fully and openly explored, to become systematized. In India, the practices and realizations of yoga are not deemed exclusively religious pursuits. Yoga is considered a science. The science of yoga addresses the various ways one may come to know reality and may ultimately achieve realization of one's oneness with God. It is an all-consuming enterprise, which very few have the inclination and discipline to pursue with the necessary dedication. Yet, as with any science, it is accepted that if one follows the proven procedures, the desired results will be achieved.

On the other hand, the mysticism of the West has been mysticism in isolation. It has not been part of the flow of a great river of awareness, as is seen in the East. Rather, there has sprung up alone, here and there, in the folds of the earth, a clear, cool spring of illumination to quench the thirst of those with an inner inclination toward the truth. The Christian theologian so blessed was typically branded a heretic, persecuted as well as prosecuted for departure from dogma. This was the case, to name a few, with St. Francis of Assisi in the thirteenth century, Meister Eckhart in the fourteenth century, Jacob Boehme in the seventeenth century, and Emanuel Swedenborg in the eighteenth century.

Emanuel Swedenborg

Emanuel Swedenborg's life is the most recent of those mentioned above, and thus most readily documented. The powers he actualized, which are latent in the rest of us, approach those of the realized beings of the East.

Emanuel Swedenborg (1688-1772) was one of the most remarkable individuals to inhabit this earth. It was his custom to learn all existing knowledge in a given field and then make an original contribution of his own. In this manner, he wrote 154 works on seventeen sciences prior to devoting his investigation solely to spiritual matters, on which he wrote an additional 282 works after the age of fifty-seven. In addition, he was a musician, an inventor, a craftsman (mastering at least seven crafts), and was fluent in nine languages (Van Dusen 1981, 195–197).

Yet these are not Swedenborg's most remarkable feats. His demonstrated powers of clairvoyance, precognition, telepathy, communication with the deceased—all well documented in the learned circles of Europe, of which he was a prominent member—are even more striking. His mastery of these capacities of the mind requires knowledge of what is, for the rest of us, the unknown. This mastery thus substantiates his comprehension of ultimate reality.

Since childhood, Swedenborg enjoyed practicing a meditative and hypnagogic technique involving the stilling of the breath. This he apparently began to do spontaneously, out of personal inclination. However, in the East, this is a well-known technique employed to enhance the depth of meditation. In India, it is one of the breathing exercises termed *pranayamas*. In China, it is called neonatal breathing, or womb breathing. This practice (when

Swedenborg began employing it much more extensively in his fifties) apparently led to his phenomenal abilities.

One day in Stockholm, for example, the gentlemen in his company decided to put Swedenborg's reputed abilities to the test. They asked him who nearby would be the next person to die. Upon agreeing to submit to their test, Swedenborg appeared to become immersed in deep meditation, after which he announced that Olof Olofsohn would die the next day at 4:45 a.m. In response, one of the gentlemen, who was a friend of Mr. Olofsohn, announced he would go to his house the following morning to see if Swedenborg's prediction occurred.

Early the next morning, while on the way to ascertain if the prediction had come true, the gentleman encountered Mr. Olofsohn's servant, who informed him that his master had just been seized by a fit of apoplexy and died. Another circumstance that attracted attention was the fact that Mr. Olofsohn's clock stopped at the moment of his death—precisely at 4:45—a circumstance we may now view as a mirror coincidence (Trobridge 1976, 204).

The credibility accorded Swedenborg by prominent intellectuals of his day, as well as in this century, is illustrated by the fact that Carl Jung's *Collected Works* includes a letter about a well-known incidence of Swedenborg's clairvoyance. The letter was written by Immanuel Kant. The letter, quoted in full below, illustrates quite well both the nature of his abilities and the circumstances in which they were witnessed:

> The following occurrence appears to me to have the greatest weight of proof, and to place the assertion respecting Swedenborg's extraordinary gift beyond all possibility of doubt.
>
> In the year 1759, towards the end of September, on Saturday at four o'clock P.M. Swedenborg arrived at Gottenburg from England, when Mr. William Castel invited him to his house, together with a party of fifteen persons. About six o'clock Swedenborg went out (to the garden), and returned to the company quite pale and alarmed. He said that a dangerous fire had just broken out in Stock-

holm, at the Södermalm (Gottenburg is about fifty German miles from Stockholm), and that it was spreading very fast. He was restless and went out often. He said the house of one of his friends, whom he named, was already in ashes, and that his own was in danger. At eight o'clock, after he had been out again, he joyfully exclaimed, "Thank God! The fire is extinguished; the third door from my house." This news occasioned great commotion throughout the whole city, but particularly amongst the company in which he was. It was announced to the Governor the same evening. On Sunday morning Swedenborg was summoned to the Governor who questioned him concerning the disaster. Swedenborg described the fire precisely, how it had begun and in what manner it had ceased, and how long it had continued. On the same day the news spread through the city, and as the Governor thought it worthy of attention, the consternation was considerably increased; because many were in trouble on account of their friends and property, which might have been involved in the disaster. On Monday evening a messenger arrived at Gottenburg, who was dispatched by the Board of Trade during the time of the fire. In the letters brought by him, the fire was described precisely in the manner stated by Swedenborg. On Tuesday morning the Royal Courier arrived at the Governor's with the melancholy intelligence of the fire, of the loss which it had occasioned, and of the houses it had damaged and ruined, not in the least differing from that which Swedenborg had given at the very time when it happened; for the fire was extinguished at eight o'clock.

What can be brought forward against the authenticity of this occurrence (the conflagration of Stockholm)? My friend who wrote this to me has examined all, not only in Stockholm, but also, about two months ago, in Gottenburg, where he was well acquainted with the most respectable houses, and where he could obtain the most authentic and complete information, for as only a very short time had elapsed since 1759, most of the inhabitants are still alive who were eyewitnesses to the occurrence. (Jung 1969, 297)

Perhaps the most famous of the many examples of Swedenborg's dialogues with the deceased was his communication to Sweden's Queen Louisa Ulrica of a message from her deceased brother. Count Höpken's account of the incident is as follows:

> Swedenborg was one day at a court reception. Her Majesty asked him about different things in the other life, and lastly whether he had seen, or had talked with, her brother, the Prince Royal of Prussia. He answered, No. Her Majesty then requested him to ask after him, and to give him her greeting, which Swedenborg promised to do. I doubt whether the Queen meant anything serious by it. At the next reception Swedenborg again appeared at court; and while the Queen was in the so-called white room, surrounded by her ladies of honour, he came boldly in, and approached Her Majesty, who no longer remembered the commission she had given him a week before. Swedenborg not only greeted her from her brother, but also gave her his (the brother's) apologies for not having answered her last letter; he also wished to do so now through Swedenborg; which he accordingly did. The Queen was greatly overcome, and said, "No one, except God, knows this secret." (Trobridge 1976, 197)

More examples of Swedenborg's phenomenal abilities could be presented if the intent was merely to entertain and engorge the curious. But since the purpose is to illustrate his capacity to transcend the limits imposed upon the rest of us, these examples should suffice, for they reveal the well-deserved credibility accorded his feats by those witnessing them and the intellectuals who appraised them. Clearly, Swedenborg's knowledge of reality must have been much deeper and more vital than that which you and I enjoy.

The Baal-Shem Tov

The Baal-Shem Tov, a relatively unknown contemporary of Swedenborg's with similar abilities, was a Hassidic master of the Kabbala. He was born in the village of Okup on the Polish-Russian border. When he was a child, the Baal-Shem's parents died. The people of Okup took it upon themselves to raise him and send him to the local religious school. Yet he preferred the surrounding forests where he would go off for days, eating nuts, fruit, and berries while delighting in nature and its creatures.

The Baal-Shem Tov had a passion for prayer, although an indifference to orthodoxy. He was very unassuming and modest, as were the circumstances of his life until his thirty-sixth year. Then, in 1734, he assumed the leadership of the Nistarium, a secret society of Kabbalists. He brought the shrouded teachings of Jewish mysticism out into the open and illustrated God's dominion by acting as a vehicle to portray God's supremacy over the apparent barriers of the world.

There are hundreds of stories about the Baal-Shem transforming lives and performing miracles. As with Swedenborg, he revealed knowledge of the life beyond death. In one well-known instance, a young man who died, and who had been skeptical of the Baal-Shem, appeared in a dream of a friend, who also doubted the Baal-Shem. In the dream, the deceased friend told of seeing the Baal-Shem in paradise, asking questions to students of the Torah. The deceased friend related a particular question that was asked, as well as the student's answer.

On the next Sabbath, the doubting dreamer visited the Baal-Shem to find him asking his disciples the very same question. The man, attempting to impress the Baal-Shem, quickly offered the answer he had received in the dream. The Baal-Shem responded that he knew it was a dead man who provided him with that answer, after which the young man became another of the Baal-Shem's disciples.

In the synagogue, the Baal-Shem's prayers would occasionally be interrupted while he entered into a state of ecstasy. At other times, he might leave the service to rush off on some urgent mission, which only he could perceive. In one such instance, he suddenly left the house of prayer to ride on horse to a nearby wood, where he rescued a woman from being murdered by her husband.

Many also witnessed miraculous visions or experienced deep mystical states in his presence. On various occasions, witnesses reported seeing the Baal-Shem surrounded by flames when he prayed. Once, after he had assured a friend whose cattle were lost that they were not stolen or dead but would return, the friend asked how he could see what was beyond sight. His answer did not differ from what one might expect from a realized master from India. He said, "God's light is hidden in the world, and whoever can find that light can use it to see from one end of the universe to the other."

When his disciples tried to forestall his imminent death through prayer, the Baal-Shem instructed them not to do so. He told them they should have no fear, concluding, "I'm only going out one door and in another" (Levy 1987, 76-84).

Before relating these examples of the capacities possessed by Swedenborg and the Baal-Shem Tov, I noted that the vivid experience of God's intimate presence in all of creation is rare in the West, where the ability to be unobstructed by the barriers of the physical world are almost unheard of. Yet in Eastern cultures, this is not the case. Such phenomena are threaded throughout the fabric of history. And even today, the strong, ingrained traditions of India germinate and nurture individuals who come to personify the ultimate truths hidden within creation.

Paramahansa Yogananda

Toward the close of the nineteenth century, the need to bring the ancient wisdom of the East to America and the West began to gain force in India. The first to travel and lecture widely in the United States was Swami Vivekananda, who initially came to address the World Parliament of Religions in Chicago in 1893. The first great saint to reside permanently in the United States was Paramahansa Yogananda, who was directed by his mentor to bring the teachings of India to the West. He came to this country in 1920.

Paramahansa Yogananda arrived in Boston, where he had been invited to address the International Congress of Religious Liberals. He established residence there prior to commencing a transcontinental tour in 1924, which was followed by the establishment of an American headquarters in Los Angeles in 1925. Yogananda was extremely successful in disseminating the knowledge that he had come to the West to present. He lectured to full-capacity crowds, sometimes numbering in the thousands. In 1927, he visited with President Calvin Coolidge in the White House. On a return trip to India in 1935, Mahatma Gandhi asked Paramahansa Yogananda to initiate him in the form of yoga that he taught his followers. After Gandhi's death, a portion of his ashes were presented to Yogananda, which he enshrined at his Lake Shrine in the Pacific Palisades section of Los Angeles, while dedicating a Mahatma Gandhi World Peace Memorial there.

Yogananda had abundantly realized his selfless goals in America, when, after residing here for over a quarter of a century and nearing the end of his earthly existence, he published the well-received and still popular *Autobiography of a Yogi*. His aim was not to advertise his own achievements, but rather to present the miraculous feats of the great men and women he had encountered in India and elsewhere in his life. This was done in recognition of the truth that Jesus declared: "Except ye see signs and wonders, ye will not believe" (John 4:48). This same recognition is the reason for inclusion of what is presented here: to lend credibility to the mystical perception of reality espoused by these individuals.

One of my favorite episodes in *Autobiography of a Yogi*—one that perhaps underscores the continuity of the emerging union of East and West—was revealed by E. E. Dickinson, one of Yogananda's longtime followers. In December of 1936, when he returned to Los Angeles after a world tour and extended visit to India, Yogananda brought with him Christmas presents for many of his much-loved followers. He presented the gifts at a joyous party on Christmas Eve. When Dickinson was handed a small rectangular box, he suddenly saw a dazzling flash of light. It was the third time in his life he had seen that same flash of light.

The first time occurred when, as a five-year-old in a small town in Nebraska, he had accidentally been pushed into a deep pond by his brother. While going under the surface for the second time, he saw a dazzling, multicolored light with the figure of a man with peaceful eyes and a reassuring smile in the middle of it. As he was going under for the third time, he was able to grab the end of a small willow tree, which his companions had bent over toward him, and thus was saved from drowning.

Twelve years later, when, as a seventeen-year-old, Dickinson was visiting Chicago with his mother, he again saw the brilliant flash of light. And there in front of him, strolling leisurely by, was the same man he had seen in the vision when the multicolored light first appeared before him. After Dickinson excitedly told his mother that it was the man who had appeared when he was drowning, they went into the large auditorium that the gentleman had entered. It was the site of the World Parliament of Religions. They saw the man seated on a lecture platform and soon learned he was Swami Vivekananda, from India, who would be speaking to the assemblage.

After they enjoyed an inspiring talk by Vivekananda, Dickinson went up to meet him. But before he could say anything, Vivekananda greeted him with the familiarity of an old friend, saying, "Young man, I want you to stay out of the water!" while smiling warmly. In his heart, the young Dickinson was hoping Swami Vivekananda would be his teacher, but didn't know how to express his ideas. Vivekananda read his thoughts, and while gazing on him with beautiful penetrating eyes, replied: "No my son, I am not your guru. Your teacher will come later. He will give you a silver cup."

Thirty-two years later, still longing for a spiritual mentor, Dickinson prayed deeply that the Lord would send him his guru. A few hours later that evening, he was awakened by glorious music while a group of heavenly beings came before his eyes carrying flutes and other musical instruments, then slowly receded. The next evening, he attended one of Paramahansa Yogananda's lectures for the first time. He was captivated by Yogananda and soon became one of his close followers.

Another eleven years passed, during which Dickinson avidly followed Yogananda's teachings, until that Christmas Eve, forty-three years after meeting Swami Vivekananda (which, as circumstance would have it, was also forty-three years after Paramahansa Yogananda was born). Vivekananda's words were but a fading memory when Dickinson received the Christmas gift from his guru and saw the flash of light for the third time. Once he opened the box, he could only utter in amazement, "The silver cup!" While withdrawing to a chair some distance away, in a dazed state of deep emotion, he simply stared at the cup, which finally fulfilled Vivekananda's forty-three-year-old prophecy. Yogananda merely went on playing Santa Claus. It was not until some time later that Dickinson was able to regain his composure sufficiently enough to relate the incredible story to Paramahansa Yogananda, which, given his abilities, one strongly suspects Yogananda was already aware of (Yogananda 1979, 543-546).

In recent years, scientists have increasingly come to appreciate the holographic nature of our physical universe; that it consists of images made up of enduring patterns of light energy, which we experience as material and solid. Our perception of reality may then perhaps best be viewed as a type of ingrained hypnosis. Michael Talbot's recent book, *The Holographic Universe*, is a synthesis of the wide spectrum of findings that point to the conclusion that matter is holographic, that, for instance, the cup you are drinking from is just a projected three-dimensional pattern of light.

In his autobiography, Paramahansa Yogananda presented the same perspective. In a chapter entitled "The Law of Miracles," he points out that God's first command in the creation of the universe, "Let there be light!" (Genesis 1:3), brought forth the structural element for creation: light. Yogananda says:

> A yogi who through perfect meditation has merged his consciousness with the Creator perceives the cosmical essence as light (vibrations of life energy); to him there is no difference between the light rays composing water and the light rays composing land. Free from the three dimensions of space and the fourth dimension of time, a master transfers his body of light with equal ease over or

through the light rays of earth, water, fire, and air. (Yoga-nanda 1979, 315)

Yogananda points out the implications of Einstein's theory of relativity, which shows time and space to be illusory, and of his proof of the equivalency of mass and energy (energy = mass times the speed of light squared), which renders the velocity of light to be the only constant. Yogananda states the implication is that "no material body, whose mass increases with its velocity, can ever attain the velocity of light. Stated another way: only a material body whose mass is infinite could equal the velocity of light." One might add, or inquire, what ultimately is the difference between a material body whose mass is infinite and a material body that is massless? Yogananda says:

> The consciousness of a perfected yogi is effortlessly iden-tified not with a narrow body but with the universal struc-ture.... He who knows himself as the omnipresent Spirit is subject no longer to the rigidities of a body in time and space.
>
> Masters who are able to materialize and dematerialize their bodies and other objects, and to move with the velocity of light, and to utilize the creative light rays in bringing into instant visibility any physical manifestation, have fulfilled the lawful condition: their mass is infinite. (Yogananda 1979, 315)

Paramahansa Yogananda was too humble to relate examples of his own powers, except occasionally the relatively commonplace abilities of knowing what is happening in other places and in other people's minds, and of accurately seeing future events. However, he did relate many instances of astounding miracles performed by other realized beings.

One of these occurred, when as a youth, he asked his father, who was a vice president of the railroad, if he could take a sight-seeing trip to Banares (Yogananda 1979, 25-29). His father promised to consider the request. The next day, his father said that, in fact, he had a business proposal he wanted to present to a friend in Banares whose address he had lost. He provided Yogananda with a pass and a letter for the friend, while instructing his son to contact another friend (for whom he gave his son a note of introduction), who was an exalted disciple of the same guru as his father. He said that the second friend, Swami Pranabananda, would likely know how to get the letter to the friend who was the prospective business partner, Kedar Nath Babu.

When he arrived in Banares, Yogananda went directly to Swami Pranabananda's residence, where he found the Swami seated in a meditative posture in a room on the second floor. Yogananda was greeted with "Bliss to my dear one," after which he inquired, "Are you Swami Pranabananda?" To this the Swami nodded and responded, "Are you Bhagabati's son?" though Yogananda had not introduced himself or provided the note his father had given him.

The Swami said that, of course, he would locate Kedar Nath Babu, after which he engaged in a few pleasantries before abruptly terminating the conversation and becoming motionless. Yogananda became somewhat embarrassed and confused as to what he should do, since he had not been informed of how to contact the other gentleman. But then the Swami said: "Little sir, do not get worried. The man you wish to see will be with you in half an hour." He then returned to his inscrutable silence.

When the young Yogananda's watch indicated thirty minutes had elapsed, the Swami suddenly informed him that he thought Kedar Nath Babu was nearing the door. In confusion and incomprehension, since the Swami had spoken to no one else, Yogananda unceremoniously left the room to go downstairs to see if in fact Kedar Nath was arriving.

He asked the gentleman he encountered if he were Kedar Nath Babu, to which the man inquired if he were Bhagabati's son, who had been waiting to meet him. Then, when Yogananda asked how he happened to come there that day, Kedar Nath responded, "Everything is mysterious today!" He explained that less than an hour prior, he had just finished bathing in the Ganges when Swami Pranabananda appeared to tell him that Bhagabati's son was waiting for him at the Swami's house, though Kedar Nath had no idea how the Swami knew where to find him. Then, after they started toward the house, the Swami asked Kedar Nath how long it would take to get there. After being told it would take about a half-hour, the Swami said he would meet him at his house, for he had something else to do. He then disappeared into the crowd ahead.

Yogananda said, "I can't believe my ears! Why that man, Swami Pranabananda, has not left my sight a moment since I first came, about an hour ago."

When they entered the room where the Swami waited, he asked them: "Why are you stupefied at all this? The subtle unity of the phenomenal world is not hidden from true yogis. I instantly see and converse with my disciples in Calcutta. They can similarly transcend at will every obstacle of gross matter." Yogananda later theorized that it was probably in an effort to stir his spiritual ardor that the Swami condescended to display his powers before him.

In his book *Autobiography of a Yogi*, Paramahansa Yogananda relates many other incredible feats of his own guru, Sri Yukteswar, and of Sri Yukteswar's guru, Lahiri Mahasaya, and other saints of India. Although Yogananda downplays his own accomplishments, the high esteem with which he is held in India, as well as in this country, is indicated by the fact that India issued a special commemorative postage stamp in his honor in 1977, on the twenty-fifth anniversary of his passing from this plane, which occurred in Los Angeles in 1952.

Sathya Sai Baba

If anyone has a need to see miracles being performed today, that need may be satisfied by visiting a Swami in India who has a huge following and is uncharacteristically uninhibited about displaying his abilities. His name is Sathya Sai Baba. He has indicated he will continue his work through the first two decades of the twenty-first century, so his authenticity should be open to observation for some time to come. In fact, he has already been investigated firsthand and at length by, among others, Dr. Erlendur Haraldsson. Haraldsson went to India a number of times over a period of years for that purpose, and wrote a book on his findings: *Modern*

Miracles: An Investigative Report on the Psychic Phenomena Associated with Sathya Sai Baba (Haraldsson 1987).

A couple of things are unusual about Sathya Sai Baba, relative to the "normal" Hindu saint. The first is how frequently, and even playfully, he has displayed his incredible talents over the past five decades. Normally, a yogi is very reluctant to display powers for two very sound reasons. The first is that there is a tendency for the witness to be distracted from the wisdom the teacher is attempting to impart—which has to do with the process of realizing one's own divinity—while instead becoming caught up in the marvels and perhaps the desire to replicate them. The second is that the enlightened individual may him- or herself get too attached with these abilities, which are but a symptom of an elevated state that may be jeopardized by becoming too enamored with them.

A key requisite of the exalted consciousness, of which these abilities are but a byproduct, is the dissolution of the ego of narrow individuality, so that the individual may know the higher, more expansive self. The danger of display is that the ego may grow too large as a result of the attention and admiration received from the feats of wonder. These are among the reasons that individuals who embody the highest wisdom are normally reluctant to exhibit these capacities openly. They repeatedly assert that one is merely the implement—the instrument in the hands of the Divine—in regard to the actions they perform.

The rationale for Sathya Sai Baba's abundance of miracles is, one would presume, the same as the previously mentioned explanation provided by Jesus: "Except ye see signs and wonders, ye will not believe,"(John 4:48) In fact, he does have a good reason for wanting the Indian people to believe, which has to do with the prospect of India's regaining its previous vitality and prosperity. Up until the eighteenth century, India was considered to be perhaps the wealthiest nation in the world. That is why Columbus was willing to risk falling off the edge of the world in order to try to reach her shores—when instead he accidentally discovered the West Indies, and America with its "Indians".

It has only been since the eighteenth century that India has not enjoyed prominence and prosperity. In gaining independence from Great Britain in 1947, India has only now begun to have an opportunity to regain its former stature. It may be no accident that the onset of Sathya Sai Baba's parade of miracles coincided with India's reclaimed independence. His role, for millions of Indians who had been confronted with a recent history of subservience to the West, may be to facilitate their rise to prosperity and self-respect by helping restore pride and confidence in the traditions of greatness this country enjoyed in the past.

This, too, may have something to do with the second unusual feature of Sathya Sai Baba's ministry. He did not undergo a gradual spiritual evolution under the guidance of an enlightened mentor, as is normally the case. The onset of his abilities was most sudden and remarkable, roughly coinciding with India's independence. As a very normal, unremarkable boy of fourteen, in the remote village of Sathya, he was bitten by a scorpion and went into a coma. Apparently, one moment he was dying, and the next he was suddenly completely recovered and in possession of astounding abilities. He immediately claimed to be the reincarnation of a great saint from the village of Shirdi by the name of Sai Baba, who had died fairly recently. In fact, it is accepted by the followers of Sathya Sai Baba that he is the reincarnation of Shirdi Sai Baba.

Sathya Sai Baba's most common miracles, which he has been performing for approximately fifty years, consist of causing objects to materialize according to his will, such as food of all kinds, including fruit that is out of season and that could not have been obtained in the remote locations where he resided. Often, he would cause entire meals to materialize for his assembled followers.

The most physically enduring of Sathya Sai Baba's creations are jewelry made of gold and precious gems, and other objects of gold, including small statues. Haraldsson was one of those to receive such a gift, which was produced the first time he met with Sathya Sai Baba.

Through an interpreter, Sathya Sai Baba was answering some questions posed to him by Haraldsson, when, at one point, he responded that "daily life and spiritual life should be grown together like a double rudraksha." Haraldsson did not understand what a double rudraksha was and asked Sai Baba to explain. Sai Baba made repeated attempts to explain through the interpreter, when finally, in an air of impatience, Sai Baba held out his hand and made a fist. A moment later, he opened it to reveal a double rudraksha, which he handed to Haraldsson.

A rudra is a small, very hard nut, esteemed for making necklaces used (much as the rosaries of Roman Catholics) for the repetition of a mantra or prayer. A double rudraksha, consisting of two rudras that have developed together and are connected as one, is rarely found.

After Haraldsson had examined the double rudraksha, so that he then knew what Sai Baba was referring to, Sai Baba asked for it back. He held it in his closed fist for a moment and then returned it to Haraldsson as a gift. The double rudraksha now was covered by two tiny gold shields on the top, and two on the bottom, which were held together by short gold chains on each side. A jeweler later informed Haraldsson that the gold was twenty-two carat.

In addition to rings with precious stones, bracelets, and necklaces, Sai Baba also occasionally materializes larger objects of gold. For these, he instructs devotees to make a small mound of sand on a riverbed or by the ocean. Then he concentrates briefly before plunging his hand in the sand to pull out the object—for example, a gold statue of a deity, over a foot in length.

Of course, Sathya Sai Baba is also adept in clairvoyance, precognition, telepathy, and telekinesis. In addition, in his early years, he would frequently dematerialize and rematerialize his body in the presence of groups of devotees. There is a hill near his early headquarters that, as sunset was approaching, Sai Baba liked to ascend with his devotees. However, on many occasions, Sai Baba would be in the midst of his devotees at the base of the hill and suddenly appear on the top of the hill, waving to them.

What is most unusual about Sathya Sai Baba is how uninhibited he has been in performing his marvels. Since he has indicated he will not pass from this plane until near the close of the second decade of the twenty-first century, anyone possessing adequate resources of time and money can go to India to investigate the truth of this account, and apparently will be able to do so for many years to come.

Bhagavan Nityananda

A more typical approach to the extraordinary was exhibited by Bhagavan Nityananda, of Ganeshpuri in Maharashtra, whose passing was in 1961. One of the greatest of saints, Nityananda did not like to draw attention to himself. He rarely spoke, except in response to devotees' requests for assistance, which he would frequently answer before the devotee was able to express the request verbally.

However, one time, when pressed to explain why he had walked across a raging river during the monsoon season when the boatman was afraid to take him across, his reply revealed how a master relates to the world. Nityananda, who would refer to himself as "this one," made the following reply:

> It is true that the Pavanje River was in flood at the time this one walked across, and that the boatman would not venture out. But it was not done with any motivation. It happened automatically—during the mood of the moment. But what is the use of all that? It only meant depriving the boatman of his half anna. One must live in the world like common men. . . . Once one is established in infinite consciousness, one becomes silent and though knowing everything, goes about as if he does not know anything. Though he might be doing a lot of things in several places, to all outward appearance he will remain as if he does nothing. He will always remain as if he is a witness to everything that goes on, like a spectator at a cinema show, and is not affected by the pleasant or the unpleasant. (Hatengdi 1984, 31)

At the risk of redundancy, I will offer one last illustration of the mastery that has been a product of the metaphysics and mysticism of the Indian culture for millennia: A gentleman from Boston related that, while in India doing research on Nityananda, he hired a taxi to take him to Ganeshpuri. The driver said that he knew the way there, for he had been to Ganeshpuri several times to receive Nityananda's blessing.

He said that the first time, after waiting in a long line for hours, he was startled to hear Nityananda tell him, "Go and bring your brother here." His brother had been blind from birth. Since the gentleman had heard of Nityananda's healing powers, the following week he brought his brother. Nityananda instructed him to leave his brother and return for him in three days. When he returned, he found that his brother could see. In another similar instance, an individual who was congenitally blind reputedly gained the use of his eyes after Nityananda had simply put two leaves from a tree over the person's eyes for a few moments.

Like Paramahansa Yogananda's guru, Bhagavan Nityananda instructed his successor, Swami Muktananda, to bring the teachings to the rest of the world. The latter subsequently established a Western headquarters in the Catskill Mountains of New York. In 1982, just before his death, Swami Muktananda passed on the full power of this ancient mystical tradition to Swami Chidvilasananda. Now principally residing in the United States, Gurumayi Chidvilasananda still frequently returns to her roots in India and also travels throughout the world, awakening seekers to their own greatness.

There are countless other examples of the abilities these individuals, and many other enlightened beings throughout history, possessed. These few cases are offered here simply to illustrate the grand potential of the human species, which a few—those at the far right of the bell curve of the degree of human development attained—have consistently achieved. And it is done to substantiate the body of knowledge these remarkable individuals traditionally espouse: knowledge of the ultimate nature of reality at the foundation of our universe. In the final chapter, it is their discernment, in concert with that of Western science, which will explain how our environment can be spontaneously shaped to furnish meaningful coincidences.

The Metaphysical
Basis of Coincidence

WE DO NOT USE the word *metaphysical* in everyday conversation, so let's clarify what it means in its present context. Metaphysics is defined as "the branch of philosophy that treats of the ultimate nature of existence, reality, and experience." However, here our investigation of the ultimate nature of reality is not limited to philosophical speculation. The attempt to furnish the metaphysical basis for the existence of meaningful coincidences employs similarities between the findings of modern physics in the West and the metaphysical perceptions derived from experience over the course of millennia in the East, particularly India.

THE WORLD AS ILLUSION

The first thing we need to do in our effort to determine the metaphysical basis of coincidences is to agree on the fact that our world differs greatly from the way we experience it. In the introduction, I furnished a few examples of the mystic's and the physicist's recognition that our daytime world resembles a dream world. In this section, I would first like to provide a sampling of the findings of modern physics that reveal the illusory nature of the world about us. Before we can ascertain how underlying reality is able to provide us with meaningful coincidences, we need to agree upon the fact that our natural and logical conceptions about the physical reality we are a part of are incorrect.

By now, most of us are familiar with science's description of the fundamental substance of all matter. Yet each time we consider it, or hear it described, we cannot help but react with some sense of disbelief. We somehow consider the conclusions of quantum mechanics (the nuclear physics of subatomic particles) to be at once both true and unreal. Our *experience* is what is real, not the truths of quantum physics. Yet even the parent of quantum physics, the classical physics of Newton, Galileo, and their successors, reveals that the world about us is immensely different from the way we perceive it.

Our everyday awareness of reality is primarily a product of our senses. Of these, our sense of sight is used most extensively to provide us with an ongoing dynamic picture of our immediate environment. But how well do our eyes reveal the true nature of the things we see? Let us take a closer look at the illusory nature of the colors that paint the picture of reality we perceive.

The sun provides plenty of illumination to distinguish our surroundings with precision and subtlety. It allows us to tell that a banana is yellow, not green, and thus ready to be eaten. It lets anyone see that the big splotch of liquid on my white shirt is blue, and thus surely not blood, although likely an indication my pen is hemorrhaging. And it allows appreciation of the radiant colors of the clouds and once-blue sky as the sun recedes from sight.

But, in reality, what we see as light, and the colors it contains, is simply electromagnetic energy. The sensory receptors in the retina of our eyes are sensitive to, and *interpret* as colors, electromagnetic energy vibrating within the limited range of cycles per second that provides wavelengths between 380 and 760 millimicrons. Lower frequencies, with longer wavelengths, provide us with infrared waves, radar waves, and at the lowest frequencies, the waves that carry television and radio transmissions. Higher frequencies furnish us with ultraviolet light, x-rays, gamma rays, and cosmic rays. So, no colors actually exist out there. As with dreams, the only place colors exist is in our minds.

Another illusion occurs every time we look at the sky on a clear night. Scientists consider the one constant in our universe to be the speed of light, 186,000 miles per second. Because of that factor and the vastness of our universe, the distance stars and galaxies are from the earth is measured in terms of how far light travels in a year.

Our little Milky Way galaxy, which is one of billions in the universe, is now considered to be, in width, the distance light travels in 300,000 years. If, for instance, last night you happened to be lying on the seashore gazing at Orion, which is a constellation in our galaxy composed of stars quite close to us, you would be looking at something a thousand light years away. If you then suddenly happened to witness the explosion of one of the stars in Orion's belt, you would be witnessing, at that moment, first hand, something in the heavens that occurred a thousand years ago. So, as time travelers, we witness the past unfolding every time we gaze at the night sky.

The illusory nature of our world is most dramatically revealed by twentieth-century discoveries in the subatomic realm of nuclear physics. The atomic structure of our world was intuited by the Greeks as early as 500 BCE, when Democritus said all things were "in reality nothing but Atoms and the Void." But it was not until 1905 that Einstein theorized that the apparently random "Brownian motion," which micron-sized particles of matter exhibit under the scrutiny of a microscope, was caused by the collision of atoms striking these particles. Einstein's proposal of how this could be experimentally verified was able to be accomplished less than a decade later, thus confirming the existence of atoms.

The area of an atom was later found to be defined by orbiting electrons, smaller "particles" that create a formidable barrier to the core of the atom by spinning around it at about six hundred miles per second. Later discoveries confirmed that the electrons and the central nucleus, and thus the atoms they make up—the tiny building blocks of our world—are not minuscule specs of some material substance, but simply knots of energy arranged in enduring patterns.

Let us take a closer look at the most immediate world we inhabit and know quite intimately—our bodies. The electron microscope reveals eerie landscapes within our own flesh. In *The Silent Pulse*, George Leonard describes what science says would be seen if the magnification could be increased still further:

> As the magnification increases, the flesh does begin to dissolve. Muscle fiber now takes on a fully crystalline aspect. We can see that it is made of long, spiral molecules in orderly array. And all these molecules are swaying like wheat in the wind, connected with one another and held in place by invisible waves that pulse many trillions of times a second.
>
> What are the molecules made of? As we move closer, we see atoms, tiny shadowy balls dancing around their fixed locations in the molecules, sometimes changing position with their partners in perfect rhythm. And now we focus on one of the atoms; its interior is lightly veiled by a cloud of electrons. We come closer, increasing the magnification. The shell dissolves and we go on inside to find . . . nothing.
>
> Somewhere within that emptiness, we know, is a nucleus. We scan the space, and there it is, a tiny dot. At last, we have discovered something hard and solid, a reference point. But no—as we move closer to the nucleus, it too begins to dissolve. It too is nothing more than an oscillating field, waves of rhythm. Inside the nucleus are other organized fields: protons, neutrons, even smaller "particles." Each of these, upon our approach also dissolves into pure rhythm. . . .
>
> Of what is the body made? It is made of emptiness and rhythm. At the ultimate heart of the body, at the heart of the world, there is no solidity. Once again, there is only the dance. (Leonard 1978, 33)

More illusions: in the same year as Einstein's paper on Brownian motion, he published a new theory on the nature of time and space, which was also subsequently confirmed. For all of us, hours sometimes seemed to fly by, while at other times moments seem to hang suspended. But our sense has been that, although our personal impression of time's passage may be illusory, time itself (as measured by a clock) does in reality flow at a constant rate. Yet Einstein's special theory of relativity asserted that even the constant rate of passage, which time of itself was thought to possess, is a fallacy; time and space are interconnected and by nature elastic and relative.

Experimental data have subsequently confirmed that, as someone or something travels faster, time, for it, actually passes slower. For instance, unstable subatomic particles, which disintegrate after a certain time length, consistently have a longer lifetime when their velocity is increased in laboratory settings. And the fact that clocks (whether mechanical clocks or atomic clocks) slow down when in motion has now been repeatedly confirmed. We are told that, if we could travel at the speed of light, time and aging would actually stand still.

One more illustration of the surprising nature of our phenomenal world should provide enough examples to establish that the components of our world are much less solid and disconnected than we normally consider them to be. Non-local connections refer to signals or connections that are, in effect, instantaneous. Einstein, among others, maintained that not only is the speed of light the only constant in the universe, but also that nothing travels faster than light, that there are no non-local connections. Niels Bohr and the so-called Copenhagen School, which was on the leading edge of quantum theory, insisted there was evidence for the existence of non-locality, for instantaneous connections between distant events. The difficulty was finding a way conclusively to resolve the question one way or another.

In 1964, John Bell, an Irishman from Belfast, came up with a mathematical theorem that proved the existence of non-locality. However, empirical verification had to wait until sophisticated technology could create the proper experimental environment. Finally, nearly twenty years later, Alain Aspect, of France, successfully amassed experimental evidence that provided verification of "instant" non-local connections between subatomic particles.

Aspect's verification of non-locality used measurements affecting the polarity of twin particles of light (photons), generated simultaneously from calcium atoms, to travel in different directions. It was found that influencing the polarity of one photon provided an immediate correlated change in its now-distant twin photon. The bottom line is that modern physics now asserts that Bell's theorem, as verified by Aspect's experiments, proves that instantaneous connections are a reality and, most significantly, that this universe thus functions as one interdependent entity, in which every part is instantly and intimately connected with the whole.

Suppose, for example, that at exactly 10:10 on a Sunday morning in late May, a nine-year-old boy in the Great Smoky Mountains of North Carolina lands a thirteen-inch brook trout; at that same moment, in southern New England, the honeybees are delighting in apple blossoms in full bloom; and in Milano, Italy, a young lover slips a ring onto his beloved's finger. The modern physics of quantum mechanics states that each of these events is vitally connected to the others.

Science now asserts that any occurrence, no matter how small, is instantly registered throughout the universe. Quantum physics maintains that, though this effect may be no more than what amounts to a ripple, science has proven that it does occur and that this universe must be viewed as one single body, in which all events are instantaneously registered on the one interconnected and interrelated whole.

So, we have seen that colors exist nowhere except inside our head; that we may travel thousands of years into the past simply by gazing at the night sky; that time may be slowed, and even suspended; that matter is not really solid, but simply energy in motion; and that, just as we can immediately travel from Tahiti to Times Square in a dream, a local event instantaneously travels throughout the universe. We have not yet determined how coincidences can spontaneously arise, but we have established that our world is much more fluid, unconventional, intimately interconnected, and malleable than we normally envision it.

In India, the illusory nature of our world has been acknowledged for thousands of years. It is perceived as the product of *maya*, which is the veiling or concealing power of God. Maya creates the cosmic illusion that the particularity and diversity of the phenomenal world are what is real, rather than the true reality that generates and pervades it.

In the last chapter, we saw that Paramahansa Yogananda asserted that the essence of the cosmos is vibrations of light energy. In fact, we have just noted that light (and the colors it contains) is simply electromagnetic energy. And, as George Leonard's magnification of the body beautifully illustrates, physical things, in reality, also consist of electromagnetic energy arranged in enduring patterns.

The universe as light (electromagnetic energy) is also supported by the book of Genesis. It commences with: "In the beginning God created the heaven and the earth. And the earth was without form, and void; and darkness was on the face of the deep. . . . And God said, let there be light: and there was light" (Genesis 1:1-3). It was not that the earth was merely unilluminated prior to the creation of light, but that it was "without form, and void." Light, then, is the substance that provides form—materiality—to the thought or image of the earth. Actually, the Hindu Vivekananda points out that the "Sanskrit word for creation, properly translated, should be projection, and not creation" (Vivekananda 1989, Vol 3, 123).

Buddhism, the most prevalent religion in the rest of eastern and central Asia, says reality for the individual is in his sense of it, rather than in the objective external world. One branch of Mahayana Buddhism, the Madhyamika, asserts that mankind is shackled by the illusion of perceiving form (rupa) when, in fact, all is void (sunyata). This void is not meant in a negative sense. The void is not literally empty, but is only void of anything that is not the one, pure, ultimately undifferentiated thing that is everywhere, in everything, without exception.

The other branch of Mahayana Buddhism, the Vijnanavada, is known in China as the Consciousness-Only school. It maintains that the entire universe resides only in the mind of the perceiver, that the individual's reality is not something objective, but consists entirely of his own internal sense impressions. Form refers to the form one is cognizant of, as conveyed by the senses, rather than some external thing. Our acknowledgment that the only place colors reside is in the mind and that our experience of physical things as solid and inert is incorrect is evidence for the Consciousness-Only perspective.

THE REALITY WITHIN THE ILLUSION

Let's begin our search for the true nature of a reality that can generate meaningful coincidences by looking at a phenomenon, known as complementarity, which has provided discoveries that are extremely unsettling to physicists. Complementarity refers to the dual manner in which the quanta (packets or "particles" of energy) that are the minute building blocks of our world manifest themselves. Always in motion, the quantum may behave like a focal *point* of energy or it may display the characteristics of a *wave* of energy spread over a greater area.

In 1905, Einstein published one additional paper, beyond the two previously mentioned, in which he identified the photoelectric effect of light. The photoelectric effect refers to the discharge of electrons from the surface of some metals when a beam of ultraviolet light is focused upon them. We discussed the fact that light consists of electromagnetic waves of energy. However, Einstein showed that the manner in which electrons are knocked out of the metal can only be explained if light consists of subatomic *particles*, which strike the metal in bullet-like fashion.

The schizophrenic character of light has subsequently been verified by other types of experiments as well. So, when waves of electromagnetic energy "shine" upon us, we are also being struck by subatomic particles, called photons. In spite of tremendous efforts to solve the mystery of the wave-particle duality, possessed not only by light but by all subatomic particles, science remains baffled by such an inexplicable co-reality.

Yet this, in itself, is not what is most unsettling. That has to do with the results of the so called, double-slit experiment, which astrophysicist John Gribbin describes as "the central mystery of the quantum world."(Gribbin 1984, 171) The double-slit experiment was devised to determine whether electrons and photons are really particles or whether they are waves.

The experiment goes something like this. A laser gun, which is adjusted so that it emits one photon of light at a time, is directed at a barrier with two slits in it. Somewhat behind the barrier is a photographic plate, which records the pattern of light that the photons fired from the laser make on it after they have passed through either one of the slits or both.

If light travels in waves, it would be spread out, passing through both slits, to strike the photographic plate in two locations in such a fashion that an interference pattern would materialize. (This interference pattern is similar to the pattern of intersecting waves one sees when two pebbles are simultaneously dropped near each other in a pool of water.) In fact, this type of interference pattern is registered on the photographic plate, thus affirming that the packets, or quanta, of light must move in a spread-out fashion.

However, if a device is set up to determine if a photon of light goes through one slit *or* the other, which light must do if it behaves like a particle rather than a wave, then, in fact, the photon is found to proceed randomly about half the time through one slit and half through the other. Nevertheless, when left to their own device, and not monitored, the pattern the individual photons register on the photographic plate over time is, instead, the wave interference pattern indicative of waves of light going through both slits simultaneously.

Theoretical physicist David Lindley makes the following observation about this phenomenon. "Each individual photon travels through the apparatus in the same way . . . in a manner that depends crucially on the existence of both slits. No matter how we work it, we have to conclude that each photon is somehow aware of the presence of the two slits rather than one." (Lindley 1996, 57) To say that a photon is "aware" of anything seems preposterous, but John Gribbin goes even further than that. He asserts (in his case using electrons rather than photons): "The electrons not only know whether or not both holes are open. They know whether or not we are watching them, and they adjust their behavior accordingly." (Gribbin 1984, 171)

Lindley ultimately suggests that, "a photon is not real until you measure it, or perhaps that it is the act of making a suitable measurement that causes a photon to be present or absent." (Lindley 1996, 61) Therefore, according to physicists, these minuscule subatomic entities are not only "aware" of, or "know," aspects of their environment, including whether they are being watched, but furthermore, they do not even exist unless they are looked at.

This sounds like science fiction, but is simply quantum mechanics. And while we noted that John Gribbin terms aspects of this situation to be "the central mystery of the quantum world," David Lindley sees it as just being typical of the "weirdness" inherent in all quantum physics. He says that "wave-particle duality is by all means an example of how quantum mechanics works, but it is just one example of the pervasive and sometimes frustrating principle that what you get is what you measure." (Lindley 1996, 55)

The lack of agreement on the meaning of phenomena and its implications on the ultimate nature of reality is characteristic of modern physics. David Horgan writes about his impression of a symposium he attended in 1992 at Columbia University, in which philosophers and physicists discussed the meaning of quantum physics:

> The symposium demonstrated that more than 60 years after quantum mechanics was invented, its meaning remained, to put it politely, elusive . . . for the most part each speaker seemed to have arrived at a private understanding of quantum mechanics, couched in idiosyncratic language; no one seemed to understand, let alone agree with, anyone else. The bickering brought to mind what Bohr once said of quantum mechanics: 'If you think you understand it, that only shows you don't know the first thing about it.'" (Horgan 1996, 91)

We have seen that scientists interpret the results of the double-slit experiment to mean that the particles, which are the minute ingredients of the things and processes of our world, are "aware," "know" if they are being observed, and vary their behavior accordingly. It would seem, then, that there is consciousness all about us in our phenomenological world. With that realization, we may be getting somewhere in our search for the metaphysical basis of coincidences. However, as David Horgan's observation above indicates, there are considerable confusion and disagreement among physicists about the implications of their findings. We might find it more profitable to return to the metaphysics of the East for an explanation of the true nature of reality.

Cosmologists and astrophysicists speak of the big bang, or a series of big bangs in accounting for the creation and dissolution of the universe or of one universe after another. Over a century ago, in regard to then-recent discoveries of science and the force that provides the big bang, Swami Vivekananda observed:

> Today we find wonderful discoveries of modern science coming upon us like bolts from the blue, opening our eyes to marvels we never dreamt of. But many of these are only re-discoveries of what had been found ages ago. It was only the other day that modern science found that even in the midst of the variety of forces there is unity. . . . All the forces, whether you call them gravitation, or attraction, or repulsion, whether expressing themselves as heat, or electricity, or magnetism, are nothing but variations of that unit energy. Whether they express themselves as thought . . . or as action . . . the unit from which they spring is called Prana (vital energy). . . . Prana is Spandana or vibration. When all this universe shall have resolved back into its primal state, what becomes of this infinite force? Do you think it becomes extinct? Of course not. If it became extinct, what would be the cause of the next wave, because the motion is going in wave forms, rising, falling, rising again, falling again? . . . At the end of a cycle, everything becomes finer and finer and is resolved back into the primal state from which it sprang, and there it remains for a time quiescent, ready to spring forth again. That is, projection. And what becomes of all these forces, the Pranas? They are resolved back into the

primal Prana, and this Prana becomes almost motionless—not entirely motionless; and that is what is
described in the Vedic sutra: "It vibrated without vibrations." (Vivekananda 1989,Vol 3, 399)

In this concise explanation of the cycles of creation (*projection*),
Vivekananda identifies one underlying vital energy (*prana*) that
becomes variously expressed in all thought and action. In China
also, one vital energy (*ch'i*) has been perceived to be inherent in all
things. Its myriad manifestations are the product of the oscillating
or vibratory interplay between its negative (*yin*) and positive
(yang) poles, differentiated in innumerable ways to form all things.

In the Sung Dynasty (960-1278), Neo-Confucianism melded the
investigation of ultimate reality with humanity's most fruitful
alignment with it, in both a personal and social context.

The primordial constituents of reality were seen to be vital energy (*ch'i*), and the principle or principles (*li*) governing its expression. In identifying ch'i as the all pervasive substance of the
universe, Chang Tsai, one of Neo-Confucianism's founders, sounds
like Vivekananda's characterization of the previous page:

> When the ch'i condenses, its light becomes manifest and
> it has form; when it disperses, its light is no longer mani-
> fest and it has no form. And yet, during its phase of con-
> densation, how can one say anything more than that this
> is a temporary condition? Or again, during its phase of
> dispersion, how can one then immediately say that it
> does not exist? Therefore, the sage who carefully observes
> only teaches that one should know the reason of visi-
> bility and invisibility, but not that of existence and non-
> existence.(Siu-chi Huang 1988, 248)

Like Vivekananda, Chang Tsai rejected the distinction of existence and nonexistence, preferring the concept of visibility and
invisibility. And, in his perception of ch'i condensing its light to
become form, we recognize Vivekananda's description of prana's
behavior and Paramahansa Yogananda's characterization of mat-

ter as light, as well as modern physicists' discovery that light and all things consist of electromagnetic energy. That Chang Tsai's grasp of reality is truly insightful is underscored by the following statement about the Great Harmony, which is his term for the Tao's expression in creation:

> The Great Harmony that is the *Tao* contains in it the principles of interaction between emerging and submerging, ascending and descending, and motion and quietude . . . Unless one knows the ceaseless and modulating activity of the sunbeams, one is not in a position to know the Great Harmony. (T'ang Chun-i 1956, 125)

It is surprising, to say the least, to discover that an individual in the eleventh century knew about the "ceaseless and modulating activity of the sunbeams." The ceaseless modulating, or vibratory nature of light waves, we know to be a modern discovery of Western science. A person in antiquity, to have perceived this, must indeed have had a very keen sense of vision.

In chapter two, physicist David Bohm's perspective that reality is *process* was cited in conjunction with our discussion of *The I Ching* as a forced directional coincidence. Bohm's theory of reality has been termed "Reality as Undivided Wholeness." It bears marked similarity to the above descriptions of reality held by the Hindu Vivekananda, and the Neo-Confucianist Chang Tsai, which, in fact, may have inspired it. Many modern physicists have expressed their indebtedness to Eastern metaphysics, with Niels Bohr, the founder of the Copenhagen School, even incorporating the Chinese yin-yang diagram in his family coat of arms.

Bohm's first appreciation of the interconnectedness of apparently independent entities resulted from work with plasma, a gas containing high concentrations of electrons and positively charged atoms. He was surprised to find that electrons acted in concert when in a plasma, as if they were part of a larger organism. Michael Talbot, in *The Holographic Universe*, describes Bohm's reaction to this phenomenon:

Although their individual movements appeared random, vast numbers of electrons were able to produce effects that were surprisingly well-organized. Like some amoeboid creature, the plasma constantly regenerated itself and enclosed all impurities in a wall in the same way that a biological organism might encase a foreign substance in a cyst. So struck was Bohm by these organic qualities that he later remarked he'd frequently had the impression the electron sea was 'alive.'" (Talbot 1992, 38)

The Holographic Universe presents a concept of reality that Bohm was the first scientist to introduce. A hologram, briefly explained, is a photograph of the interference pattern of a split laser beam, one-half of which proceeds directly to the photographic plate, while the other half is first reflected off some object before being registered on the plate. The image on the plate looks like nothing more defined than a puddle into which a handful of pebbles had just been tossed. Yet when a laser beam is shone through it, a realistic three-dimensional image of the photographed object materializes in space.

There are two characteristics of the hologram that are particularly surprising. The first is that what appears to be a random, unintelligible wave interference pattern, actually has encoded within it the precise three-dimensional image of some object, which may be extracted from it (when laser light is shone upon it to form the image in space). The second is more remarkable: if the photograph is cut into pieces, each piece, when illumined, will project the entire object photographed. Every part of the interference pattern on the photograph contains a record of the entire object photographed. In other words, the whole is contained in every part. The only thing that is lost when the photograph is cut into smaller pieces is clarity.

Bohm saw these characteristics of the hologram as replicating reality. He identified the key feature of the hologram to be that, "in each region of space, the order of a whole illuminated structure is 'enfolded' and 'carried' in the movement of light. Something similar happens with a radio wave. In all cases, the content or meaning that is 'enfolded' and 'carried' is primarily an order and a measure, permitting the development of a structure." (Bohm 1980, 150) Bohm called the reality that is enfolded throughout "the implicate order." The specific reality extracted or unfolded from the implicate order at any particular time and place to become the visible world he termed "the explicate."

The reality that exists when observed or measured, such as the particle when sought in the double-slit experiment and the world about us, is then but the unfolded portion of the vast implicate structure of the holomovement, which contains the patterns of all reality from the beginning of time. The constant flow of reality from the implicate order to the explicate, and then back to the ocean of the implicate, like waves advancing and retreating on a shoreline, provides the many variations of the one ocean of reality, manifested over time, in both atoms and the cosmos.

The fact that, as with the hologram, the one whole in implicate form exists in every part of reality provides an explanation for the instantaneous non-local connections that were discussed in the first section of this chapter. It is not two distinct things that are connected, but aspects of the one whole.

Bohm sees a connection between consciousness and the physical matter of the observed world. Both are aspects of the holomovement, the implicate order that has become explicate. Bohm's view, which is that matter is a less subtle form of consciousness, is then quite logical. He believes, according to Talbot, "the basis for any relation between the two lies not in our own level of reality but deep down in the implicate order. Consciousness is present in various degrees of enfoldment and unfoldment in all matter, which is why plasmas possess some of the traits of living things. As Bohm puts it, 'The ability of form to be active is the most characteristic feature of mind, and we have something that is mindlike already with the electron.'" (Talbot 1992, 50) These, I might add, are the same mind-like qualities that we saw the electron display earlier in the double-slit experiment.

The concept that our world has holographic properties, that it is a shadow-like projection of a deeper reality, is not a totally new perspective. We can see it in Sir Arthur Eddington's oft-quoted statement of well over half a century ago:

> The frank realization that physical science is concerned with a world of shadows is one of the most significant advances. In the world of physics we watch a shadowgraph performance of the drama of familiar life. The shadow of my elbow rests on the shadow table as the shadow ink flows over the shadow paper. It is all symbolic, and as a symbol the physicist leaves it. Then comes the alchemist Mind who transmutes the symbols. The sparsely spread nuclei of electric force become a tangible solid; their restless agitation becomes the warmth of summer; the octave of ethereal vibrations becomes a gorgeous rainbow. (Eddington 1929, xvii)

Eddington goes on to assert that "the stuff of the world is mindstuff" (Ibid, 276). Now we are getting close to the foundation of coincidence. Bohm believes consciousness is present in all matter. And indeed, components of atoms display intelligent behavior. If we are living in a sea of consciousness, the mechanics of coincidence could be easier to comprehend. In fact, in India all creation has long been perceived as pure consciousness.

Vivekananda's description of the dynamic prana energy, as *spandana* or vibration, and its quiescent state after and before projection as "vibrating without vibrations" are key perceptions of Hindu metaphysics. Quantum physics has also found all dynamic energy to be vibratory. However, in amplifying Vivekananda's characterizations of the vital prana energy, we may do just as well to return to the theology of the West. The Gospel according to John commences with: "In the beginning was the Word, and the Word was with God, and the Word was God" (1:1).

According to Genesis, "in the beginning God created the heaven and the earth," and this was done (as I read it) by bringing it forth—by projecting it—with light. Here, on the other hand, we are told, "in the beginning was the Word." Yet this is not a contradiction. The Word was before creation, for not only was the Word with God, but the Word *was* God.

What is this Word that is God? What is a word? A word is a representation of a thought. A word, whether spoken or thought of, is the same as the thought it represents. Very briefly, let us look at Plato, Swedenborg, and Vivekananda in regard to the significance of the Word. This is done to illustrate the true meaning and the key role of the Word in creation, in both the Hindu and the Judeo-Christian comprehension.

In his introduction to *The Republic of Plato*, Francis Cornford notes platonic philosophy's "twin pillars are the belief in a world of intelligible Forms or 'Ideas' existing independently of the things we see and touch, and the belief in an immortal soul existing in separation from the body, both before birth and after death" (Cornford 1945, xxvii). Plato's "'Ideas,' existing independently of the things we see and touch," is the same as the "Word of God" that St. John speaks of. Swedenborg says, "the Word interiorly is spiritual and celestial, therefore it was written by pure correspondences. . . . Each and all things in nature correspond to spiritual things; and in like manner each and all things in the human body" (Warren 1975, 98). In different words, Swedenborg reiterates Plato's perspective; there is a spiritual archetype that the Word expresses, and that receives further expression in the phenomena of the natural world. Vivekananda provides further clarity:

> A name is said to be very sacred. In the Bible we read that the holy name of God was considered sacred beyond compare, and it was thought that this very Word was God. This is quite true. What is this universe but name and form? Can you think without words? Word and thought are inseparable. Try if any one of you can separate them. Whenever you think, you are doing so through word forms. The one brings the other: thought brings the word, and the word brings the thought. *Thus the whole universe is, as it were, the external symbol of God, and behind that stands His grand name* [italics mine]. (Vivekananda 1989, Vol. 2, 41)

Now, with this understanding of what is meant by "the Word was God"—that the Word as God's thought, God's consciousness, is an aspect of God—we can go back to the Hindu comprehension of creation, and the deep reality projected as our world. Creation begins with the state at the end of Vivekananda's account two pages ago (the state between big bangs), when the primal energy is almost motionless, "It vibrated without vibration." But what is the nature of this vibration?

We might look to humanity for one aspect of this vibration. At the end of the chapter on symbols, we saw that Jung, Swedenborg, and Eckhart (among many others) view humanity to be the microcosm within which the macrocosm is contained and reflected. Furthermore, Genesis tells us that God made "man" in God's image. Physics, and the Hindu metaphysics Vivekananda speaks of, sees all phenomena as dynamic patterns of vibrating waves of energy. The electroencephalograph reveals that thoughts, too, are waves of energy.

Similar to the biblical pronouncement that "In the beginning was the Word," Hinduism says of the divine power: "Its essence is Self-Consciousness. It is also known as the Supreme Word (Para Vac)" (Singh 1990, 16). This Supreme Word, from which all creation emanates, is articulated as *aum*, or *om*. The saint Sri Ramakrishna described *aum* as being like the sound of a bell. With the Hindu perspective of *aum* as the primordial sound that brings forth creation, perhaps we can envision the universe as the inside of a cavernous bell and all its complex creations as the product of dynamic interference patterns of the waves of force (sound).

We have seen that both the Bible and Hinduism explain creation in terms of light and in terms of sound. What both light and sound have in common is their inherent and essential vibratory wave nature. This is the same vibratory expression of energy that physics concludes is inherent in all phenomena.

It was noted above that the essence of divine power is self-consciousness. This is the key to comprehending how reality can generate meaningful coincidences, so we should delve a little deeper into Hinduism's recognition of the role of divine consciousness.

Aum, the primordial word cited above, from which creation

proceeds, is associated with a trinity of gods. The *Ah* sound that *begins* the word is associated with Brahma, the creator. The *U* sound that is sustained in the middle is associated with Vishnu, the sustainer. And the *M*, which brings about the cessation of sound, is identified with Shiva, the destroyer.

Shiva's destroyer role is the product of his definitive attribute, absolute consciousness. That which Shiva's absolute consciousness destroys is maya's illusory power. Shiva's embodiment of supreme consciousness places him in the most exalted position; for consciousness is the foundation of creation, the reality inherent within creation, and that which transcends creation. And in destroying the illusion of maya's potency, consciousness quells the illusion of the power of the world created and sustained, respectively, by Brahma and Vishnu. According to this concept, Shiva is clearly superior to the other two. Kashmir Shavism's *Doctrine of Recognition* says, "The many powerful gods, including Vishnu and Brahma, reside within the sphere of Maya and owe their divine status to a mere spark of Shiva's power." (Dyczkowski 1992, 95)

Kashmir Shavism, which venerates Shiva as the embodiment of supreme consciousness, may perhaps be viewed as a kind of a New Testament in Hinduism to the Old Testament of Vedanta, the foundation of Hinduism. Kashmir Shavism perceives creation as the product and process of Shiva directing his supreme consciousness toward himself—as Shiva's *self*-consciousness projected on the screen of his own being, in order to witness himself. Thus, as supreme consciousness, Shiva is at once the constant reality that transcends creation, as well the creator, and the one reality inherent in creation. Shiva is thus both the conveyor and destroyer of maya's illusory power.

The liberation of the sage, such as those presented in chapter four, is founded upon the intimate knowledge of this one essence, supreme consciousness, in all diversity. The illusory power of maya, which provides the apparent solidity, separateness, and dissimilarity of the physical world, no longer holds him or her in its powerful grip.

Gold may be molded and shaped to form various bracelets, rings, necklaces, wristwatches, statuettes, pendants, earrings, etc.

They are all different, yet they all consist of nothing but gold. Similarly, the one substance which is differentiated to form all creation, and which lies beyond creation, is pure consciousness. Speaking of Shiva's absolute consciousness, Abhinavagupta says:

> The light is one, and it cannot ever be divided, and for this reason there is no possible division capable of sundering the non-duality, the Lord, beautiful with light and bliss. But (someone might object) space, time, forms, knowledge, qualities, attributes, distance, and so on are usually considered to be diversifying elements. Not so (we reply), because that which so appears is nothing but the light. If the light were not such, then non-duality would be useless. Difference then is only a word devoid of reality. But even if we admit a portion of reality to differences, then according to what we have said, it will have its basis only in non-duality. This is a pot, this is a cloth, the two are different one from the other. The two are different from other cognizing subjects, the two are different even from me. All these notions are nothing but the one light, which by its own intrinsic nature displays itself in this way. (Mueller-Ortega 1989, 97)

The light is consciousness. God is absolute consciousness. When he desires to know himself, his self-consciousness is manifested in creation. We can find parallels in meditation. In the deepest level of meditation, no self-consciousness exists. Consciousness alone exists, conscious of bliss. The next level brings consciousness of one's own self as the blissful one, perceived in all things without exception. This is akin to God when his self-consciousness arises. However, with God (absolute consciousness), the self he is conscious of is spontaneously projected on the screen of his being, which is partially perceived by us as our reality. One might say that God's consciousness congeals as our world, or as David Bohm would say, becomes explicate as our world. Yet to say that all phenomena is the expression of God's absolute consciousness still leaves much unsaid about the relationship between consciousness and coincidence. This will be explained in the following section, in which we arrive at the metaphysical basis of coincidence.

THE PHILOSOPHER'S STONE FOUND: CONSCIOUSNESS AND COINCIDENCE

The concept of the philosopher's stone is ancient and appears in diverse cultures. It maintains that there is an original indestructible substance, or ultimate principle, of which all things and phenomena are variations. Furthermore, the manifold qualities of things—that are but differentiations of this elementary material—may be penetrated to arrive at this original undefiled source. Therefore, one who is successful in penetrating to this primordial, pure, undifferentiated core, from which the visible world emanates, holds the secret of all creative power.

In Jung's *Man and His Symbols*, M. L. von Franz tells us,

> "Medieval alchemists, who searched for the secret of matter in a pre-scientific way, hoping to find God in it, or at least the working of divine activity, believed that this secret was embodied in their famous "philosophers stone." But some of the alchemists dimly perceived that their much-sought-after stone was a symbol of something that can be found only within the psyche of man." (von Franz 1964, 210)

Speaking of this same "prima materia" and "elixir of life," Lama Anagarika Govinda informs us:

> There was a group of mystics in India who applied this principle to their own spiritual development and declared that he who could penetrate to the origin and ultimate principle of unity within himself, would not only transform the elements of the external world, but those of his own being. And in doing this, he would obtain that miraculous power . . . that is equally effective in the spiritual as in the material world. (Govinda 1960, 57)

As illustrated, for instance, by the uninhibited display of miracles by Sathya Sai Baba described in chapter four, mystics with these abilities are not simply a reputed phenomenon of the past. The capacity for such transformation is quite viable today. On the other hand, von Franz's statement that the philosopher's stone was something "that can be found only within the psyche of man" should not be taken literally. No doubt what is meant was that it is not a specific substance that could be found in some particular location outside of man, such as in the earth or from some plant. For, of course, all that is within humankind must be found beyond humankind, in the source from which humankind stems.

By now, the nature of this primordial, indestructible entity that is the source of all things and activities, and the common focus of Western physics and Eastern metaphysics should be apparent. The conclusion of quantum physics, and of Eastern philosophies before it, is that the source and stuff of reality, of all creation, is consciousness. God's supreme consciousness is the metaphysical basis of coincidence. These mysteriously meaningful coincidences are arranged by the power of God's absolute consciousness, which, in fact, creates our entire universe—a universe that is the self expression of that consciousness.

The most comprehensive metaphysical portrait of the role of consciousness is the one perceived by Kashmir Shavism: the ultimate and eternal reality is absolute consciousness. Creation is the projection of the light of God's self-consciousness, the product of God's desire to be conscious of, to perceive, himself. God is everywhere, fully present in the one light of his self-consciousness, for this light of consciousness is projected on God's own being, while being differentiated in myriad ways to form all things and processes in creation.

Directional coincidences, then, are the spontaneous arrangement of particular components of consciousness in the visible world simply brought about by the force of the intention, or will, of the divine self-conscious being—of God—to guide the development of the specific nucleus of consciousness that is the individual encountering it. That, in a nutshell, is all that needs to be said about the metaphysics of directional coincidences.

Mirror coincidences are a little more complex, since they are generated by the individual. To explain them, we need to delve into human consciousness. The best way to depict individual consciousness may be to use an analogy in which the various levels of consciousness are depicted as a series of concentric spheres.

The surface level is the working *consciousness* of the waking state. It is connected by a bioelectric field of force with the concentric layers beneath it. The closest layers comprise the subconscious. The material in the *subconscious* is accessible with varying degrees of ease or difficulty to the surface consciousness. In the waking state, there is a continual exchange of data between the conscious and subconscious level, a process in which portions of consciousness recede to the subconscious, while particular subconscious elements reemerge to consciousness. The quantity of material in the subconscious is tremendously greater than that which resides in the consciousness of the individual.

The command of this process is maintained by the ego, which receives inputs from both the external and internal environment. The core of the ego resides just below consciousness in the subconscious. However, the ego maintains powerful lines of force throughout both the subconscious and conscious levels of awareness. The ego's concern is the preservation, health, and aggrandizement of the organism in which it resides.

A great many concentric layers of consciousness lie below the subconscious. They constitute by far the largest portion of individual consciousness. These comprise the *unconscious*, which retains a record of everything that has ever been seen, heard, or experienced in any form by the individual. This even includes events which never made an impact on the surface conscious level of awareness, but were only noted subliminally as they slipped into some recess of the unconscious. It includes innumerable events extending to earliest childhood, which have long ago been "forgotten." The material in the unconscious is very difficult to retrieve to consciousness. It usually makes itself felt, if at all, only in subtle and vague ways. Information from it or the impact of the information it contains generally only receives fairly direct expression in dreams. And even then, this information is likely to be conveyed in quite symbolic form.

Hidden deep within the many layers of consciousness resides the self. The self is the enduring being. The surface layers of the self are adjacent to the deepest unconscious, which contains a record of the previous lifetimes of the individual. At its core (hidden deep within the many layers of the conscious, subconscious, unconscious, and previous life records) is the vital component of the highest being: supreme self-consciousness, a component of that which is projected to become all creation of all time. And at the very heart is the state of being that is the bliss of absolute consciousness.

These layers of personal consciousness, with the Divine at the core, is our true nature. This is the miracle each of us is. So what, then, are mirror coincidences? How do we have the capacity to arrange our environment spontaneously to reflect our concerns, so that our surroundings become our psychophysical arena?

Essentially, it is that we become, in a sense, *idiot savants*. By definition, an idiot savant is "a feeble-minded individual who has unusual ability in one or more specialized activities." When it comes to mirror coincidences, that is how we function.

Many of us have read about or have seen television programs that feature an idiot savant. The mentally deficient individual might have incredible musical abilities, such as the capacity to play a song or musical score on the piano from memory after having heard it only once. Or the person may have amazing mathematical abilities, may be able to calculate instantly the day of the week that coincides with any specific date extending to the distant future or past, or may be able to calculate mentally the square root of any number. In regard to mirror coincidences, we have such an incredible ability, far beyond our normal capacity in other areas, except that, unlike the true idiot savant, it is infrequently exercised, and even then it is not under our command.

Our idiot-savant capacity to restructure our psychophysical world is simply a product of the intense concern or desire that is always associated with mirror coincidences. The concentration of force associated with a charged complex sometimes causes a direct channel to penetrate the layers of consciousness to the imbedded omnipotent self within. That spark of God within—the spark of God's omnipotent consciousness—then allows itself to be exercised to spontaneously realign pertinent portions of our environment to be aligned with the concern.

Imagine the numerous layers of consciousness that obscure our true self to be dense layers of clouds. It is as if the intense concentration of the psychological state causes a narrow beam of particularly focused dynamic energy to penetrate all the layers of clouds, like a beam of sunlight, all the way to the omnipotent self-consciousness within. According to its rules for the game of creation, this spark of the Divine remains hidden within unless the obscuring layers of personal consciousness are penetrated, which is no easy task. When the intense, focused energy of the psychological concern causes a narrow avenue to penetrate to the self, a specific ray of the divine light then shines forth, to spontaneously rearrange the area of the environment appropriate to the concern. This area thus becomes the psychophysical manifestation of the psychological concern.

So, in this brief account, we can see that the same force provides us with both directional coincidences and mirror coincidences. This force is simply the omnipotent expression of God's self-consciousness. In the first case, we and our life space are bathed in the light of that unfolding consciousness to facilitate the growth of that small portion of the infinite consciousness we each are. In the second case, the intensity of our state sometimes opens a narrow conduit to that same consciousness, which, in its omnipresence, is also hidden deep within us.

Since I have relied upon their knowledge and provided examples of those beings who have realized the Divine within, it might be appropriate to explain briefly the process they bring to fruition to avail themselves consistently of that hidden resource, the divine self within. In amplifying Shiva's "I-consciousness" earlier, we noted that parallels can be found in the stages of meditation. It is this process of meditation that serves to dissipate the intervening clouded layers of consciousness that enclose the radiant and transforming light of the true self.

When deep meditation is consistently practiced over a long period of time, the ego of the small self gradually atrophies and eventually dies, while the levels of consciousness associated with it lose their massive, forceful nature, which previously blocked contact with the deeper levels of transcendent consciousness.

Once the level of pure consciousness is reached, the limited self is shed in the processes of the blossoming of a pure universal ego, in which one's self is known to be the consciousness that is manifest in all things. This brings to mind a definition of humans and God provided by Vivekananda:

> Man is an infinite circle whose circumference is nowhere, but the center is located in one spot; and God is an infinite circle whose circumference is nowhere, but whose center is everywhere. He works through all hands, sees through all eyes, walks on all feet, breathes through all bodies, lives in all life, speaks through every mouth, and thinks through every brain. Man can become like God and acquire control over the whole universe if he multiplies infinitely his center of self-consciousness. Consciousness, therefore, is the chief thing to understand. (Vivekananda 1989, Vol 2, 33)

For humans to become aware that they are the "infinite circle" Vivekananda speaks of, they each must become one of those extremely rare individuals who has realized his or her fullest potential for development. Mark Dyczkowski says of the exalted state of this self-realized being:

> He knows that he is one with all embodied beings and that his physical body is not his true nature but an externally perceivable form, separate and yet one with him, like a reflection in a mirror. Identification of 'I' consciousness with the limited locus of his body thus naturally shifts to

the unlimited expanse of the All which he now experiences as his true body. (Dyczkowski 1992, 41)

Dyczkowski's assertion that the self-realized individual experiences the "unlimited expanse of the All" as his true body *is* meant literally. Just as we command our personal physical bodies to perform the functions we desire to have accomplished, the person who has realized divine consciousness may command his or her cosmic nature to perform what he or she wills.

Bhaskara's commentary on aphorism 22 of the Shiva Sutras amplifies this capacity as follows:

The unconditioned light of consciousness which illumines every manifestation is pure. 'Knowledge' is the enlightened consciousness that 'I am all things.' It is said to be the awareness of that light which, because it emits all the countless things that exist, possesses the highest possible degree of freedom. The vision of the light is the arising of Pure Knowledge through which the yogi attains the perfection which is the expanding development of the sovereign power (of consciousness) and the mastery of the Wheel of Energies. (Dyczkowski 1992, 57)

The freedom, power, and mastery spoken of here are over the visible world emitted by the light of consciousness.

There is one last topic I would like to discuss in this investigation of coincidence. That is the question of the validity of the law of cause and effect, for it possesses important implications on the significance of coincidences. The foundations of the physical cosmos we inhabit are space, time, and causality. Space and time are certainly relative, and there are deep mysteries in the cause of phenomena; however, modern physics' assertion that the flow of events is the product of probability is flawed. All activity is lawful.

In 1927, Werner Heisenberg published a paper in which he said there is an inherent uncertainty in the relationship of events to each other. The *uncertainty principle* has had a tremendous impact on physics and influence in other fields as well, particularly philosophy. It is a product of experimental limitations that exist when physicists attempt to measure the position and momentum of an electron and of limitations in the equations physicists used to predict the behavior of subatomic particles.

The particles of light (photons) that must be used to photograph the position of another particle (electron) disrupt the momentum of the electron by impacting with it. Therefore, the physicist can never know both the position and momentum of subatomic particles. Consequently, the physicist cannot predict with certainty the effect that the experimenter's observation will have on the particle. The statistical probability of various subsequent positions and momentums is all that may be determined. The bottom line is that, according to physicists, we can no longer maintain that one event causes a particular effect; the most that can be done is to calculate the statistical *probability* of subsequent activity.

Heisenberg said, "We cannot know, as a matter of principle, the present in all it details." (Gribbin 1984, 257) The difficulty I have is that scientists insist that the inability to know an electron's position and momentum is not due to experimental limitations (in essence saying that the apparatus and the equations used are the best there will ever be), but that the uncertainty about the behavior of our world is due to "a fundamental truth about the nature of the universe."(Ibid, 158)

It is logically inconsistent, if not impossible, to declare a fundamental truth about the nature of the universe, when one asserts one does not have the ability to know the nature of that universe. The current inability to demonstrate causality's operation in the subatomic realm does not rule out its operation there, nor does it mean that what occurs there and in the conventional world is intrinsically uncertain, and thus can only be viewed as a matter of statistical probability. In fact, David Cassidy points out that Heisenberg did not consider the uncertainty principle to be applicable to the world at large: "Quantum mechanics, he argued, contains a fundamental statistical element, but the element is not a property of nature itself—rather, it enters with the physicist's examination of nature." (Cassidy 1992, 234)

Another challenge to causality's status is associated with the fact that, in the traditional cause-and-effect framework, the effect must follow that which caused it. The existence of non-local connections, which was discussed in the first section of this chapter, proved that an event in one place was associated with an instantaneous response elsewhere. This naturally gives rise to the assertion that, if they both occur simultaneously, one event cannot be said to cause another. But, for instance, does not moving the base of a pool cue forward cause the simultaneous movement of the tip of the cue? Perhaps the parameters of the law of cause and effect simply need to be redefined.

In regard to both the events in our universe and the fate of individuals, nothing happens by chance. Meteorologists are still a long way from being able to predict the weather accurately. Yet, although they forecast in terms of the probability of precipitation, they do not maintain its occurrence is the product of chance. Albert Einstein may not have been right about everything. But regardless of fellow physicists' certainty about uncertainty, when he asserted that "God does not roll dice," he was right on.

Nothing that happens to us is fortuitous. It reflects the past history and present activity of that particular ray of absolute consciousness that, in effect, the individual is, and it conforms to the compassionate consciousness of God. The color, clarity, and ease with which the ray of light that is you travels through eternity is influenced by how harmoniously you respond to the one impelling force of consciousness that directs all creation. If we respond openly and intelligently to the guidance provided, our journey can be one of contentment and bliss.

Bibliography

Barks, Coleman. 1997. *The Essential Rumi.* Edison, N.J.: Castle Books.

Berendt, Joachim-Ernst. 1987. *Nada Brahma: The World is Sound.* Rochester,Vt.: Destiny Books.

Blakney, Richard B. 1941. *Meister Eckhart: A Modern Translation.* New York: Harper & Row.

Bohm, David. 1980. *Wholeness and the Implicate Order.* Boston: Routledge & Kegan Paul.

Capra, Fritjof. 1991. *The Tao of Physics.* Boston: Shambhala Publications, Inc.

Cassidy, David C. 1992. *Uncertainty: The Life and Science of Werner Heisenberg.* New York: W. H. Freeman and Company.

Chan, Wing-Tsit. 1963. *A Source Book in Chinese Philosophy.* Princeton, N.J.: Princeton University Press.

Chun-i, T'ang. 1956. "Chang Tsai's Theory of Mind and Its Metaphysical Basis." *Philosophy East And West* 6.

Cirlot, J. E. 1962. *A Dictionary of Symbols.* Tr. Jack Sage. New York: Philosophical Library, Inc.

Cornford, Francis MacDonald. 1945. *The Republic of Plato.* New York: Oxford University Press.

Dyczkowski, Mark. 1992. *The Aphorisms of Shiva.* Albany, N.Y.: State University of New York Press.

Eddington, Sir Arthur. 1929. *The Nature of the Physical World.* New York: McMillin Company.

Govinda, Lama Anagarika. 1960. *Foundations of Tibetan Mysticism.* New York: E. P. Dutton & Co.

Gribbin, John. 1984. *In Search of Schrodinger's Cat.* New York: Bantum Books.

Hall, Calvin, and Gardner Lindzey. 1963. *Theories of Personality.* New York: John Wiley & Sons, Inc.

Haraldsson, Erlendur. 1987. *Modern Miracles: An Investigative Report on Psychic Phenomena Associated with Sathya Sai Baba.* New York: Fawcett Columbine.

Hatengdi, M. U. 1984. *Nityananda: The Divine Presence.* Cambridge, Mass.: Rudra Press.

Herbert, Nick. 1985. *Quantum Reality, Beyond the New Physics.* New York: Anchor Press/Doubleday.

Horgan, John. 1996. *The End of Science.* Reading, Mass.: Addison-Wesley Publishing Co.

Huang, Siu-chi. 1988. "Chang Tsai's Concept of Ch'i." *Philosophy East And West.* Vol. 18.

Jung, C. G. 1959. *The Collected Works of C. G. Jung.* Vol. 10. Princeton, N.J.: Princeton University Press.

———. 1966. *The Collected Works of C. G. Jung.* Vol. 15. Princeton, N.J.: Princeton University Press.

———. 1969. *The Collected Works of C. G. Jung.* Vol. 18. Princeton, N.J.: Princeton University Press.

———. 1973. *Synchronicity.* Princeton, N.J.: Princeton University Press.

Koestler, Arthur. 1972. *The Roots of Coincidence.* New York: Random House.

Lau, D. C. 1989. *Tao Te Ching.* Hong Kong: The Chinese University Press.

Leonard, George. 1978. *The Silent Pulse.* New York: E.P. Dutton.

Levy, Edward. 1987. *Darshan.* Vol. 9. South Fallsburg, N.Y.: SYDA Foundation.

Lindley, David. 1996. *Where Does The Weirdness Go.* New York: Basic Books.

Mitchell, Stephen. 1988. *Tao Te Ching.* New York: Harper & Row.

Muller-Ortega, Paul. 1989. *The Triadic Heart of Shiva.* Albany, N.Y.: State University of New York Press.

New Haven Register. 1996. *Nation,* May 27. Los Angeles Times News Service.

Peat, F. David. 1987. *Synchronicity: The Bridge Between Matter and Mind.* New York: Bantam Books.

Singh, Jaideva. 1990. *The Doctrine of Recognition.* Albany, N.Y.: State University of New York Press.

————. 1992. *The Yoga of Vibration and Divine Pulsation.* Albany, N.Y.: State University of New York Press.

Suzuki, D. T. 1996. *Swedenborg: Buddha of the North.* West Chester, Pa.: The Swedenborg Foundation.

Talbot, Michael. 1981. *Mysticism and the New Physics.* New York: Penguin Books.

————. 1992. *The Holographic Universe.* New York: Harper Collins Publishers, Inc.

Trobridge, George. 1976. *Swedenborg: Life and Teachings.* New York: Harcourt Brace Jovanovich, Inc.

Trungpa, Chogyam. 1984. *Shambhala: The Sacred Path of the Warrior.* New York: Bantam Books.

Van Dusen, Wilson. [1972] 1981. *The Natural Depth in Man.* New York: The Swedenborg Foundation.

————. 1988. "A Mystic Looks at Swedenborg." *Emanuel Swedenborg: A Continuing Vision.* Ed. Robin Larsen et. al. New York: The Swedenborg Foundation.

Vaughan, Allen. 1979. *Incredible Coincidence.* New York: J. B. Lippincott Co.

Venkatesananda, S. 1993. *Vasistha's Yoga.* Albany, N.Y.: State University of New York Press.

Vivekananda, S. 1989. *The Complete Works of Swami Vivekananda.* Calcutta, India: Advaita Ashrama.

von Franz, Marie-Louise. 1992. *Psyche and Matter*. Boston: Shambhala Publications, Inc.

Warren, Samuel M., ed. 1975. *A Compendium of the Theological Writings of Emanuel Swedenborg*. New York: Swedenborg Foundation.

Wilhelm, Richard. 1967. *The I Ching*. Tr. Cary F. Baynes. Princeton, N.J.: Princeton University Press.

Yogananda, Paramahansa. 1979. *Autobiography of a Yogi*. Los Angeles: Self Realization Fellowship.

Index

China, xiii, 59, 72, 91, 98; Sung
Dynasty, 184
ch'i, (vital energy), 184
chit, 66
Chuang Tzu, xvi
Cirlot, J.E., *A Dictionary of Symbols,* 133–134
clocks, xviii; in coincidence, 5,
156. *See also* watch
coincidence: defined, xii, 6, 7n,
45-47;
interpreting meaning of, 13–14,
46–47, 129–130
complementarity, 180
complex: defined, 10; as magnet,
9–12, 27, 28; symbols in association with, 12
Confucianism, 91
Confucius, 112
consciousness, xvi; connection
with physical matter, 187;
as foundation of the world,
188–192, 192, 198–199;
in subatomic particles,
181–182, 183
Consciousness-Only school of
Buddhism, 179
conservation of symbols. *See*
symbols, conservation of
contentment, 144–152
Coolidge, Calvin, 161
Copenhagen School, 177, 185
Cornford, Francis, *The Republic
of Plato,* 189
correspondence theory, 39,
133–136
crucifixion of Jesus. *See* Jesus of
Nazareth
cup, symbolic meaning of, 115–121

D
darkness, symbolic meaning of,
118

death, and mirror coincidence, 5,
156
déjà vu, 30
Democritus, 175
Dickens, Charles, 29
Dickinson, E. E., 161–163
Dionysius, St., 88, 89
directional coincidence: defined,
xv; examples of, 58–75;
life-saving, 12, 42–44;
metaphysical basis of, 194,
197; romance and, 48–58;
this book and, 75–91
Doctrine of Recognition, 191
double-slit experiment, 180–182
dreams, xiii; conservation of
symbols in, 69–70, 125–129;
reflected in coincidences,
29–31; similarities with coincidence, xv, xvi, xvii, 8, 29–31
Dyczkowski, Mark, 198–199

E
Eckhart, Meister, 88–90, 105,
1900; benefit of deferring to
God's will,121–122, 151;
nature's symbols, 136–137
Eddington, Sir Arthur, 188
Einstein, Albert: Brownian
motion of atoms, 175;
complementarity (photo-
electric effect of light), 180;
and dice, xvii, 201; non-local
connections, 177;
relativity, theory of, 177
Eldorado, 55–57
electrons, 175, 176, 180–182,
consciousness possessed by,
181–182; lifelike activity, 186
elixir of life, 193
*Emanuel Swedenborg:
A Continuing Vision,* 40, 41

L
Lao Tzu, 72, 73
Last Supper, the, 115–118
Leonard, George, *The Silent Pulse,* 176, 179
li, (principle), 184
life, as dreamlike, xiii, xvi, xvii, 31
life-saving coincidences, 12, 42–44
light, nature of, 174–175, 177, 178, 179; Abhinavagupta and, 192; the Baal-Shem Tov and, 160; biblical account of, 179; Chang Tsai and, 184,185; Paramahansa Yogananda and 163–164
Lindley, David, 181–182

M
macaw, golden, 39, 40
Madhyamika branch of Buddhism, 179
Magnus, Albertus, 25, 26
Mahayana Buddhism, 179
Manhattan, 53
Mansur al'Hallaj, 119
maya, 179, 191
Mecca, 119
meditation, 192, 197–198
Michigan, 126
Milky Way (galaxy), 175
mind as magnet, 21, 24–28. *See also* complex, as magnet
mirror coincidence: defined, xv; metaphysical basis of, 195–197; role of, 5–6, 36–37
monk: Korean, 60–64, 91; Trungpa Chogyam, 70
Muktananda, Swami, 171
Mustang (automobile), 9, 10, 123
mysticism, xviii; mystical experience defined, 40–41; validity of mystic's apprehension of reality, 153–155

N
Native American, 68–69, 89
near-death experience, 136
needs, xix, 82
Neo-Confucianism, 184
neonatal breathing, 155
Nityananda, Bhagavan, 170–171
non-locality of subatomic particles, 177–178
nuclear physics, xviii. *See also* quantum physics
numbers as symbols, 40, 122, 123

O
Orion, constellation of, 175

P
Parker, Richard, ix
peach, as symbol for the heart, 72, 73, 75
Peale, Norman Vincent, *The Power of Positive Thinking,* 143
Peat, F. David, *Synchronicity: The Bridge between Mind and Matter,* 15, 16
perfection, divine, 148
persona, 128
Peter (disciple of Jesus), 118
philosopher's stone, 193–194
Phoenix, 89, 90
physics: classical, 174. *See also* quantum physics
plasma, David Bohm's findings about, 185–186
Plato, 135, 189
plum, 73, 75
Poe, Edgar Allen, ix
positive visualization, 143; and mirror coincidence, 144
prana, (vital energy), 183–184
Pranabananda, Swami, 165–166
pranayama, 155

unconscious, the, 62, 65–66
Union of Soviet Socialist
    Republics, 59

V

Van Dusen, Wilson: "A Mystic
    Looks at Swedenborg," 40, 41;
    The Natural Depth in Man, 40
Vietnam, Cam Rahn Bay Air
    Base, xii, 58, 59
Vijnanavada, branch of Bud-
    dhism, 179
Vishnu, 191
Vivekananda, S., 184, 185; con-
    sciousness, 198; God and man
    defined, 198; E. E. Dickinson
    and, 162–163; symbolic nature
    of universe, 137; universe as
    projection, 179; universal
    force in the universe, 183–184,
    188; word as the universe, 189
von Franz, Marie-Louise, 30, 31,
    193

W

Wagner, Richard: *The Ride of the
    Valkyries,* 108

War: Second World, ix–x;
    Vietnam, 58, 59
warriorship, 64, 70–71, 87–91
watch: in coincidence, 3–5, 16;
    symbolic meaning of, 5
Wheeler, John, xvii
Wilhelm, Richard: *The I Ching,*
    93, 94, 96, 98, 103, 103n
wine, as symbol, 115–117
womb breathing, 155
world, as illusion, 173–180
World War II, ix–x

Y

yin and yang, 61, 62, 63, 66, 184,
    185
Yoga Vasistha, xvi
Yogananda, Paramahansa, 120;
    Autobiography of a Yogi,
    160–166; on theory of relativi-
    ty, 164; universe as light,
    163–164